Trevor McDonald's World of Poetry

TREVOR MCDONALD'S
World of Poetry

Trevor McDonald
with illustrations by Molly Sample

ANDRE DEUTSCH
CLASSICS

First published in Great Britain in 1999
By André Deutsch Classics
76 Dean Street
London W1V 5HA
www.vci.co.uk

Selection and introduction © 1999 Trevor McDonald
Illustrations © 1999 Molly Sample
For copyright in individual poems, see the poetry acknowledgements
at the back of the book

CIP data for this title is available from the British Library

ISBN 0 233 99511 0

1 3 5 7 9 10 8 6 4 2

Jacket design by Kee Scott Associates
Typesetting by Derek Doyle & Associates, Liverpool
Printed and bound by MPG Books, Bodmin, Cornwall

For Jack and his cousin, Ryan Grant

Introduction

Anthologies have always been a source of fascination to lovers of poetry. Of course they mean different things to different people, but there's fairly broad agreement amongst poets themselves on what ALL anthologies should do. John Betjeman suggested that the range of any selection of poems should be sufficiently wide to make the reader sit up, marvel, listen and want to hear more. Betjeman went on to say they should even want to hear the words read out loud.

W.H. Auden felt that anthologies should inspire the reader to embark on a journey of discovery and exploration, allowing him or her to walk through the vast, magical expanse of the world of poetry, stopping off here and there to admire the style, the subtle tones and the overall beauty of the language. I think Auden and Betjeman say it all. Anthologies should excite and charm, they should delight and challenge, they should be enjoyed for their sheer variety and they should help us to recall the wonderful language of glorious lines sometimes sadly forgotten. They should inform, and of course they should educate.

No anthology can claim to be the poetic equivalent of the Bible, nor would we wish to give the impression that this is the definitive collection. But it's my hope that it will appeal to all lovers of poetry and language. Having said that, this anthology is also aimed at those who, regardless of age, might be coming to poetry for the first time. In this context I hope that the bibliographical notes provided will not only be informative but will act as a rough navigational chart, encouraging readers to find out more about the extraordinary, and in many instances the bizarre, lives of some of the most brilliant and famous poets. This, above all, should commend the book to younger readers whose growing interest in poetry is making the art more popular than it ever was.

Two other points on the way the book is organised. It will be necessary for readers to skip about to find poems by the same author, but I do hope that any inconvenience caused by this is outweighed by the intrigue, the sense of adventure and the endless surprises to be found in turning the pages. Also, as in all the best anthologies, the book's two indexes, on poets and first lines, should make it terribly easy to find any poem.

The main discipline in compiling an anthology is to make sure that the book is not made up entirely of one's favourite poems. Indeed, in making any selection it is difficult to avoid one's favourites. For me that difficulty was real enough. I was brought up on poetry and have always loved it. My parents were my first teachers and they used poems they knew to reinforce the moral and social values they were taught and the ones they attempted to pass on to their offspring. Thus I was constantly reminded that:

> Lives of great men all remind us
> We can make our lives sublime,
> And, departing, leave behind us
> Footprints on the sands of time;

The message of those lines was inescapable. I should do well at school, become a model citizen and leave my mark on the community in which I was brought up. My parents' deeply religious outlook was underscored by lines from Tennyson:

> More things are wrought by prayer
> Than this world dreams of. Wherefore, let thy voice
> Rise like a fountain for me night and day.
> For what are men better than sheep or goats
> That nourish a blind life within the brain,
> Both for themselves and those who call them friend?

The seed of love poetry once sown bore rich pickings for me and I hope that is obvious in the choices I have made for this anthology. They will, as you will see, range from Shakespeare, Keats and Shelly to Auden and Larkin and the West Indian poet Derek Walcott, who with such pointed elegance describes the dilemma of Afro-Caribbeans like me who were born in the English West Indies and who crossed the Atlantic to live in what was the Mother Country. In his poem, A Far Cry From Africa, he says:

> I who am poisoned with the blood of both,
> Where shall I turn, divided to the vein?
> I who have cursed
> The drunken officer of British rule, how choose
> Between this Africa and the English tongue I love?

I do hope that in this selection I have roamed far beyond simply my favourites to satisfy the greatest variety of poetic tastes and persuasions.

Some poems have been cut because they are too long for this one and for most anthologies, but far from being the cause of annoyance, I trust that this will do no more than incite those interested to read more widely.

The greatest virtue of poetry, like all branches of literature, is that it spans all time, peoples, languages and cultures. It defines what and who we are and clarifies and distils our deepest thoughts. Poetry is, in reality, a part of us all and one reason for its immense richness and its never-ending hold on all civilisations is that it truly belongs to the world. It is a part of our heritage we must never forget.

Trevor McDonald

Acknowledgements

Having already acknowledged the debt I owe to my parents, and particularly my mother for my interest in poetry, I would like to express my gratitude to all those people who continually write to me about it and to whose letters, inquiries, comments and insights, I have not always been able to respond. Where I have managed to reply to letters, I am acutely aware that my responses have not always been adequate, insightful or even helpful. I apologise.

I began discussing this book with Michèle Brown of André Deutsch and her many suggestions and her tremendous enthusiasm were an enormous help. On the inevitably more practical business of actually producing the book and deciding over many weeks what should be included and what should be left out, sometimes by our deciding and on many other occasions by the will of others, I shall be always grateful to Stephanie Goodwin. She manages to combine in the precisely correct proportions the admirable ability to encourage and support with the more obviously important consideration of making sure that deadlines are met. I am indebted to her.

When I talked about doing this book, my family gave me nicely stern lectures about how good it should be. I can only hope that they are not disappointed. Their admonitions were entirely instructive. Errors and obvious ommissions are down to me.

ALFRED, LORD TENNYSON
1809–1892

Crossing the Bar

Sunset and evening star,
   And one clear call for me!
And may there be no moaning of the bar,
   When I put out to sea,

But such a tide as moving seems asleep,
   Too full for sound and foam,
When that which drew from out the boundless deep
   Turns again home.

Twilight and evening bell,
   And after that the dark!
And may there be no sadness of farewell,
   When I embark;

For tho' from out our bourne of Time and Place
   The flood may bear me far,
I hope to see my Pilot face to face
   When I have crost the bar.

Tennyson was a best-selling poet and friend of Queen Victoria. His poems are often romantic but he was also interested in science, religion and social problems. The death of his closest friend Arthur Hallam, when both were still young men, inspired Tennyson to write more than a hundred poems about grief and all the questions it brings. These were published in 1850 under the title In Memoriam.

This poem was composed in twenty minutes while Tennyson was crossing the strip of water known as the Solent, near the Isle of Wight. This was one of Tennyson's favourite coastal landscapes and in old age he requested that it be published at the end of all collections of his poetry.

WILLIAM BLAKE
1757–1827

The Lamb

Little Lamb, who made thee?
　Dost thou know who made thee?
Gave thee life & bid thee feed,
By the stream & o'er the mead;
Gave thee clothing of delight,
Softest clothing woolly bright;
Gave thee such a tender voice,
Making all the vales rejoice!
　Little Lamb who made thee?
　Dost thou know who made thee?

Little Lamb I'll tell thee,
　Little Lamb I'll tell thee!
He is callèd by thy name,
For he calls himself a Lamb:
He is meek & he is mild,
He became a little child:
I a child & thou a lamb,
We are callèd by his name.
　Little Lamb God bless thee.
　Little Lamb God bless thee.

———————————

Blake is often described as a man who did not belong to his own age.
Working as an artist and poet, based in London, he published his own
hand-made books which did not reflect the artistic fashions of the time. He
was suspicious of Sir Isaac Newton's theories about the universe, but as he
got older he came to accept scientific discovery.

　He still preferred, though, to take a more mystical view of the way in
which things are made. In his book Songs of Innocence Blake
emphasizes the importance of freedom and joy in a child's life. This simple
poem about a lamb reminds the animal that he was created by God. There

2

is an echo, too, of Jesus being referred to as 'The Lamb of God' in the New Testament. In Blake's original publication the text of the poem is set within an illustration of leafy trees and a child feeding a lamb.

ROBERT GRAVES
1895–1985

Counting the Beats

You, love, and I,
(He whispers) you and I,
And if no more than only you and I
What care you or I?

Counting the beats,
Counting the slow heart beats,
The bleeding to death of time in slow heart beats,
Wakeful they lie.

Cloudless day,
Night, and a cloudless day;
Yet the huge storm will burst upon their heads one day
From a bitter sky.

Where shall we be,
(She whispers) where shall we be,
When death strikes home, O where then shall we be
Who were you and I?

Not there but here,
(He whispers) only here,
As we are, here, together, now and here,
Always you and I.

Counting the beats,
Counting the slow heart beats,
The bleeding to death of time in slow heart beats,
Wakeful they lie.

---

*Robert Graves was a brilliant and complex writer who suffered shell-shock
in the First World War and who recorded the horror of what he saw in his*

autobiography Goodbye to All That. *He spent many fascinating and turbulent years living in Deya on the island of Majorca. Most of his poetry is about romantic love. He thought that men frequently lost touch with the instinct of love, and that they needed women or muses to help them to rediscover love and to write about it.*

WILLIAM SHAKESPEARE
1564–1616

Sonnet 18

Shall I compare thee to a summer's day?
Thou art more lovely and more temperate.
Rough winds do shake the darling buds of May,
And summer's lease hath all too short a date:
Sometime too hot the eye of heaven shines,
And often is his gold complexion dimm'd;
And every fair from fair some time declines,
By chance, or nature's changing course, untrimm'd;
But thy eternal summer shall not fade
Nor lose possession of that fair thou ow'st;
Nor shall Death brag thou wand'rest in his shade,
When in eternal lines to time thou grow'st.
   So long as men can breathe or eyes can see,
   So long lives this, and this gives life to thee.

———————————

William Shakespeare is the greatest English playwright of all time. He wrote over 150 sonnets which have intrigued readers for centuries. They were probably only intended for circulation among his closest friends, and perhaps he never wanted them published, but they did appear in print in 1609. Some people think that the sonnets are a kind of autobiography of Shakespeare's love affairs although no one knows for sure. None of the characters in the sonnets is given a name, except for the poet.

The first seventeen sonnets are concerned with encouraging a good-looking young man to marry and have children so that his beauty will be passed on to the next generation. In sonnet 18, however, the poet is expressing his love for the man in question. The poet declares that the poem itself will ensure the immortality of the man's beauty.

WILLIAM WORDSWORTH
1770–1850

She Was a Phantom of Delight

She was a Phantom of delight
When first she gleamed upon my sight;
A lovely Apparition, sent
To be a moment's ornament;
Her eyes as stars of Twilight fair;
Like Twilight's, too, her dusky hair;
But all things else about her drawn
From May-time and the cheerful Dawn;
A dancing Shape, an Image gay,
To haunt, to startle, and way-lay.

I saw her upon nearer view,
A Spirit, yet a Woman too!
Her household motions light and free,
And steps of virgin-liberty;
A countenance in which did meet
Sweet records, promises as sweet;
A Creature not too bright or good
For human nature's daily food;
For transient sorrows, simple wiles,
Praise, blame, love, kisses, tears, and smiles.

And now I see with eye serene
The very pulse of the machine;
A Being breathing thoughtful breath,
A Traveller between life and death;
The reason firm, the temperate will,
Endurance, foresight, strength, and skill;
A perfect Woman, nobly planned,
To warn, to comfort, and command;
And yet a Spirit still, and bright
With something of angelic light.

Wordsworth was born in Cumberland and his most famous poetry is concerned with the landscape of the Lake District. He was a friend of the poet Coleridge and a supporter of the French Revolution. Wordsworth did not care for glamour or fashion, and believed that walking in the countryside and reflecting on the natural world around us gave us the strength, both to cope with our own lives and to view others with sympathy. He hated writing his poems on paper, and composed them by humming out the rhythm to himself. Once he thought of the words, he often dictated his poems to his sister Dorothy.

WILFRED OWEN
1893–1918

Dulce Et Decorum Est

Bent double, like old beggars under sacks,
Knock-kneed, coughing like hags, we cursed through sludge
Till on the haunting flares we turned our backs
And towards our distant rest began to trudge.
Men marched asleep. Many had lost their boots
But limped on, blood-shod. All went lame; all blind;
Drunk with fatigue; deaf even to the hoots
Of tired, outstripped Five-Nines that dropped behind.

Gas! Gas! Quick, boys! – An ecstasy of fumbling,
Fitting the clumsy helmets just in time;
But someone still was yelling out and stumbling
And flound'ring like a man in fire or lime . . .
Dim, through the misty panes and thick green light,
As under a green sea, I saw him drowning.

In all my dreams, before my helpless sight,
He plunges at me, guttering, choking, drowning.

If in some smothering dreams you too could pace
Behind the wagon that we flung him in,
And watch the white eyes writhing in his face,
His hanging face, like a devil's sick of sin;
If you could hear, at every jolt, the blood
Come gargling from the froth-corrupted lungs,
Obscene as cancer, bitter as the cud
Of vile, incurable sores on innocent tongues,—
My friend, you would not tell with such high zest
To children ardent for some desperate glory,
The old Lie: Dulce et decorum est
Pro patria mori.

FRANCIS BRETT YOUNG
(1884–1954)

Prothalamion

When the evening came my love said to me:
Let us go into the garden now that the sky is cool;
The border of black hellebore and rosemary,
Where wild woodruff spills in a milky pool.

Low we passed in the twilight, for the wavering
Heat of the day had waned;
Around that shaded plot of secret beauty the thickets clustered
    sweet:
Here is heaven our hearts whispered, but our lips spoke not.

Between that old garden and seas of lazy foam
Gloomy and beautiful alleys of trees arise, with
Spikes of cypress and dreamy beeches dome,
So dark that our enchanted sight knew nothing
But the skies,
Veiled with a soft air, drenched in the roses musk or
The dusky, dark carnation's breath of clove:

No stars burned in their deeps, but through the dusk
I saw my love's eyes, and they were brimmed with love.
For doves that crooned in the leafy noonday, now
Were silent; the night jar sought his secret cover, a
Mild sea whisper moved a creaking bough.
Was ever a silence deeper made for lovers?

Was ever a moment meeter made for love?
Beautiful are your close lips beneath my kiss; and all
Your yielding sweetness beautiful – oh, never in all
The world was such a night as this!

W.H. AUDEN
1907–1973

Funeral Blues

(IX of Twelve poems)

Stop all the clocks, cut off the telephone,
Prevent the dog from barking with a juicy bone,
Silence the pianos and with muffled drum
Bring out the coffin, let the mourners come.

Let aeroplanes circle moaning overhead
Scribbling on the sky the message He Is Dead,
Put crêpe bows round the white necks of the public doves,
Let the traffic policemen wear black cotton gloves.

He was my North, my South, my East and West,
My working week and my Sunday rest,
My noon, my midnight, my talk, my song;
I thought that love would last for ever: I was wrong.

The stars are not wanted now: put out every one;
Pack up the moon and dismantle the sun;
Pour away the ocean and sweep up the wood;
For nothing now can ever come to any good.

───────────

Auden was born in York, England, but emigrated to the United States in 1939 – the year the Second World War began. His poems are often concerned with morality, politics and our sense of responsibility for people and for the world around us.

CHARLES OLSON
1910–1970

III. Spring

From Variations Done for Gerard Van De Wiele

The dogwood
lights up the day.

The April moon
flakes the night.

Birds, suddenly,
are a multitude

The flowers are ravined
by bees, the fruit blossoms

are thrown to the ground, the wind
the rain forces everything. Noise –

even the night is drummed
by whippoorwills, and we get

as busy, we plow, we move,
we break out, we love. The secret

which got lost neither hides
nor reveals itself, it shows forth

tokens. And we rush
to catch up. The body

whips the soul. In its great desire
it demands the elixir

In the roar of spring,
transmutations. Envy

drags herself off. The fault of the body and the soul
– that they are not one –

the matutinal cock clangs
and singleness: we salute you

season of no bungling

Olson was born in Massachusetts, in the United States and did not become interested in writing poetry until he was in his mid-thirties. Like fellow American e e cummings, his poetry was influenced by the music and the art of his time. In Olson's case that meant jazz and abstract expressionist painting.

DANTE GABRIEL ROSSETTI
1828–1882

Sonnet: Dante Alighieri to Guido Cavalcanti

Guido, I would that Lapo, thou, and I,
Led by some strong enchantment, might ascend
A magic ship, whose charmèd sails should fly
With winds at will where'er our thoughts might wend,
So that no change, nor any evil chance
Should mar our joyous voyage; but it might be,
That even satiety should still enhance
Between our hearts their strict community:
And that the bounteous wizard then would place
Vanna and Bice and my gentle love,
Companions of our wandering, and would grace
With passionate talk, wherever we might rove,
Our time, and each were as content and free
As I believe that thou and I should be.

(trans. Percy Bysshe Shelley)

JOHN MILTON
1608–1674

How Soon Hath Time

How soon hath Time, the subtle thief of youth,
   Stoln on his wing my three and twentieth year!
   My hasting days fly on with full career,
   But my late spring no bud or blossom shew'th.
Perhaps my semblance might deceive the truth,
   That I to manhood am arrived so near,
   And inward ripeness doth much less appear,
   That some more timely-happy spirits endu'th.
Yet be it less or more, or soon or slow,
   It shall be still in strictest measure even
   To that same lot, however mean or high,
Toward which Time leads me, and the will of Heaven;
   All is, if I have grace to use it so,
   As ever in my great Taskmaster's eye.

John Milton was a learned man who read widely and, in addition to his poetry wrote many pamphlets and essays on political, social and religious issues. Paradise Lost *is perhaps his best-known work, described by John Dryden as 'one of the greatest, most noble and sublime poems which either this age or nation has produced'.*

There is much discussion surrounding Milton's personality. Described as good-natured and sociable, he has also been labelled a tyrant, domestic bully, strict Puritan and misogynist. His achievements are all the more impressive, however, when one considers that by 1652, at the height of his career, he had become completely blind.

WILLIAM COLLINS
1721–1759

Ode Written in the Beginning of the Year 1746

How sleep the brave who sink to rest
By all their country's wishes blest!
When Spring, with dewy fingers cold,
Returns to deck their hallowed mould,
She there shall dress a sweeter sod
Than Fancy's feet have ever trod.

By fairy hands their knell is rung,
By forms unseen their dirge is sung;
There Honour comes, a pilgrim grey,
To bless the turf that wraps their clay
And Freedom shall awhile repair,
To dwell a weeping hermit there!

Collins is considered one of the first poets of the Romantic Movement. These poets were more interested in expressing feelings than concentrating on poetic form. Collins suffered from ill-health and depression all his life. He was influenced by the Latin poet Horace and by writers like Shakespeare, Spenser and Milton. This poem suggests that the spring brings comforting thoughts about the renewal of life.

Early in 1746 Bonnie Prince Charlie was making a claim to the throne of England. He was a Scottish Catholic whose army suffered a terrible defeat at the Battle of Culloden in April 1746. Although the poem makes no reference to historical events it is likely that Collins was well aware of Bonnie Prince Charlie's desire to alter the course of history.

ROBERT BROWNING
1812–1889

Lines from The Pied Piper of Hamelin

I

Hamelin Town's in Brunswick,
   By famous Hanover city;
The river Weser, deep and wide,
Washes its wall on the southern side;
A pleasanter spot you never spied;
   But, when begins my ditty,
Almost five hundred years ago,
To see the townsfolk suffer so
   From vermin, was a pity.

II

   Rats!
They fought the dogs and killed the cats,
   And bit the babies in the cradles,
And ate the cheeses out of the vats,
   And licked the soup from the cooks' own ladles,
Split open the kegs of salted sprats,
Made nests inside men's Sunday hats,
And even spoiled the women's chats
     By drowning their speaking
     With shrieking and squeaking
In fifty different sharps and flats.

III

At last the people in a body
   To the Town Hall came flocking:
' 'Tis clear,' cried they, 'our Mayor's a noddy;
   'And as for our Corporation – shocking
'To think we buy gowns lined with ermine
'For dolts that can't or won't determine
'What's best to rid us of our vermin!
'You hope, because you're old and obese,

18

'To find in the furry civic robe ease?
'Rouse up, sirs! Give your brains a racking
'To find the remedy we're lacking,
'Or, sure as fate, we'll send you packing!'
At this the Mayor and Corporation
Quaked with a mighty consternation

———————————

Browning was married to the popular poet Elizabeth Barrett Browning. His own work was highly regarded but it was considered more difficult to understand. He loved Italy and some of his poems feature characters from the late Italian Renaissance (sixteenth-century Italy). Browning was also a playwright.

He wrote this poem for a little boy called Willie, the son of William Macready who was an actor and theatre manager. Willie was not at school because he had a bad cough and wanted to be kept busy. He had a talent for drawing, so Browning wrote the poem and sent it to him to illustrate. Willie did not forget to send Browning a thank you letter and copies of his pictures.

In the first three verses of the poem, Browning describes the rat infested town of Hamelin and of how the townspeople call upon the Mayor and Corporation to rid them of this vermin. Their answer is to employ the Pied Piper to charm the creatures away for a sum of a thousand guilders.

VII

Into the street the Piper stept,
   Smiling first a little smile,
As if he knew what magic slept
   In his quiet pipe the while;
Then, like a musical adept,
To blow the pipe his lips he wrinkled,
And green and blue his sharp eyes twinkled,
Like a candle-flame where salt is sprinkled;
And ere three shrill notes the pipe uttered,
You heard as if an army muttered;
And the muttering grew to a grumbling;
And the grumbling grew to a mighty rumbling;
And out of the houses the rats came tumbling.

———————————

Though he has freed the town of rats the Mayor and Corporation refuse to pay the thousand guilders promised and the Piper is forced to punish them by using his pipe to charm the town's children away to the hills.

XV

So, Willy, let me and you be wipers
Of scores out with all men – especially pipers!
And, whether they pipe us free fróm rats or fróm mice,
If we've promised them aught, let us keep our promise!

ANDREW SALKEY
b. 1928

Dry River Bed

he came back
by plane,
train,
bus
and cart

his expectations
were plain:
family,
eyecorner familiarity,
back-home self,
or so he thought

1
during the last stretch,
on foot,
over the hard dirt road,
a beggar smiled at him,
and held out his left hand,
like a reaping hook

he gave him
nearly all his small change

2
further along the way,
a tatter of children
offered him pebbly mangoes,
at a price

he handed over
the rest of his change,
without taking the mangoes

3
on the narrative veranda,
where all the village tales
had perched
and taken off again,
his mother stood,
as light as the money
he'd just given away

in his embrace,
her body, wrapped wire,
felt smaller
than he remembered,
her face drawn tight
and frightened

4
everything was diminished,
whittled by long urban knives:
the road outside,
the front garden,
the lean-to house,
the back yard,
the lives

5
all his family
and neighbours
were knocking softly
at death's door,
waiting patiently,

spit fringing their cracked lips,
wizened frowns
sliding
into their collapsed cheeks

6
the villagers clawed at him
and what little he'd brought back,

they picked him clean
as a eucalyptus

7
he quickly saw
that home was a dry river bed;
he knew he'd have to run away, again,

or stay and be clawed to death
by the eagle
hovering over the village;
nothing had changed

8
he walked alone,
for a while;
not even his footprints
sank behind him,
in the dust;

no niche,
no bounce-back,
no mirror, anywhere,
in which to see himself,
merely the sunlight
mocking everybody, everywhere,
and the circling eagle

W. S. RENDRA
b. 1935

The Moon's Bed, the Bride's Bed

The moon's bed, the bride's bed:
An azure blue sky
Held up by ancient hands;
A cricket flutters about,
Shrilling a love song to the net.

The moon's bed, the bride's bed:
A Chinese junk with a thousand sails
Crossing the sea of sleep;
Stars fall one by one,
Yawning with sweet visions.

The moon's bed, the bride's bed:
A kingdom of ghosts and spirits,
Drunk with the flavour of incense;
Dreams scatter, one by one,
Cracked by brittle truth.

(trans. Burton Raffel)

Rendra was born in the Javanese town of Solo, Indonesia. He was brought up a Christian but his poetry also refers to the traditional Javanese faith. As an adult Rendra became a Muslim. He writes about relationships and emotions.

This poem suggests that the dreams people have about their married life will eventually disappear.

GEOFFREY CHAUCER
ca. 1343–1400

The Canterbury Tales

Lines from The General Prologue

Whan that April with his° showres soote°	*its / sweet*
The droughte of March hath perced to the roote,	
And bathed every veine in swich° licour,°	*such / liquid*
Of which vertu engendred is the flowr;	
Whan Zephyrus eek° with his sweete breeth	*also*
Inspired hath in every holt° and heeth°	*grove / field*
The tendre croppes,° and the yonge sonne	*shoots*
Hath in the Ram his halve cours yronne,	
And smale fowles maken melodye	
That sleepen al the night with open yë° –	*eye*
So priketh hem° Nature in hir corages –	*them*
Thanne longen folk to goon° on pilgrimages,	*go*
And palmeres for to seeken straunge strondes	
To ferne halwes, couthe° in sondry londes;	*known*
And specially from every shires ende	
Of Engelond to Canterbury they wende,	
The holy blisful martyr for to seeke	
That hem hath holpen° when that they were seke.°	*helped / sick*

Chaucer was the first poet to write literature in English. He did not use the modern spellings we know today but what was called 'Middle English'. Before that, Latin was thought to be the language appropriate for poetry, while official documents at the court of the English king were written in French. Chaucer was a royal poet, a soldier, a judge, an MP and a customs house controller, so he encountered a great variety of people through his work.

The Canterbury Tales *remained his most famous work. England was a Roman Catholic country at this time and Chaucer tells the tales of a group of twenty-nine pilgrims who meet at an inn in Southwark (south London) the night before they walk to the shrine of Thomas à Becket in Canterbury, Kent. They decide to tell stories on the walk and to award the best storyteller with a free supper at the inn on their return. The lines above set the scene by describing spring, the season for pilgrimages.*

ROBERT GRAVES
1895–1985

It Was All Very Tidy

When I reached his place,
The grass was smooth,
The wind was delicate,
The wit well timed,
The limbs well formed,
The pictures straight on the wall:
It was all very tidy.

He was cancelling out
The last row of figures,
He had his beard tied up in ribbons,
There was no dust on his shoe,
Everyone nodded:
It was all very tidy.

Music was not playing,
There were no sudden noises,
The sun shone blandly,
The clock ticked:
It was all very tidy.

'Apart from and above all this,'
I reassured myself,
'There is now myself.'
It was all very tidy.

Death did not address me,
He had nearly done:
It was all very tidy.

They asked, did I not think
It was all very tidy?

I could not bring myself
To laugh, or untie
His beard's neat ribbons,
Or jog his elbow,
Or whistle, or sing,
Or make disturbance.
I consented, frozenly,
He was unexceptionable:
It was all very tidy.

CHARLES WOLFE
1791–1823

The Burial of Sir John Moore

Not a drum was heard, not a funeral note,
  As his corse to the rampart we hurried;
Not a soldier discharged his farewell shot
  O'er the grave where our hero we buried.

We buried him darkly at dead of night,
  The sods with our bayonets turning;
By the struggling moonbeam's misty light,
  And the lantern dimly burning.

No useless coffin enclosed his breast,
  Not in sheet or in shroud we wound him;
But he lay like a warrior taking his rest,
  With his martial cloak around him.

Few and short were the prayers we said,
  And we spoke not a word of sorrow;
But we stead fastly gazed on the face that was dead,
  And we bitterly thought of the morrow.

We thought, as we hollowed his narrow bed,
  And smoothed down his lonely pillow,
That the foe and the stranger would tread o'er his head,
  And we far away on the billow!

Lightly they'll talk of the spirit that's gone,
  And o'er his cold ashes upbraid him, –
But little he'll reck, if they let him sleep on
  In the grave where a Briton has laid him.

But half of our heavy task was done,
  When the clock struck the hour for retiring;
And we heard the distant and random gun
  That the foe was sullenly firing.

Slowly and sadly we laid him down,
    From the field of his fame fresh and gory;
We carved not a line, and we raised not a stone –
    But we left him alone with his glory!

━━━━━━━━━━

Wolfe was born in Ireland and worked as a curate in Donoughmore. He died of consumption, when he was very young, and after the woman he loved refused his proposal of marriage. He only wrote fifteen poems, by far the most famous of which is 'The Burial of Sir John Moore'.

Sir John Moore (1761-1809) was a British lieutenant general who fought against the Americans in their war of independence and against Napoleon's French forces. He was mortally wounded in a battle with French soldiers and buried at midnight in Corunna, in Spain. Wolfe had no first-hand experience of such fighting and he based his poem on a prose account of Moore's death published in the Annual Register. *Byron praised the poem but doubted that it was really written by Wolfe, because he didn't think such a little-known poet could have written such a powerful and accomplished poem.*

WENDY COPE
b. 1945

The Uncertainty of the Poet

I am a poet.
I am very fond of bananas.

I am bananas.
I am very fond of a poet.

I am a poet of bananas.
I am very fond,

A fond poet of 'I am, I am' –
Very bananas,

Fond of 'Am I bananas,
Am I?' – a very poet.

Bananas of a poet!
Am I fond?' Am I very?

Poet bananas! I am.
I am fond of a 'very'.

I am of very fond bananas.
Am I a poet?

———————————

Wendy Cope has worked as a primary school teacher and finds that children's interest in creative writing encourages her to write. She began writing poetry in 1973, after the death of her father, and is a frequent and well-known contributor to popular newspapers and magazines.

SIR WALTER RALEGH
1554–1644

Three Things There Be

Three things there be that prosper all apace,
    And flourish while they are asunder far;
But on a day, they meet all in a place,
    And when they meet, they one another mar.

And they be these; the Wood, the Weed, the Wag:
    The Wood is that that makes the gallows tree;
The Weed is that that strings the hangman's bag;
    The Wag, my pretty knave, betokens thee.

Now mark, dear boy – while these assemble not,
    Green springs the tree, hemp grows, the wag is wild;
But when they meet, it makes the timber rot,
    It frets the halter, and it chokes the child.

God Bless the Child!

———————————

Ralegh was a famous military and naval commander who headed exploratory voyages to South America and other distant lands. He was a favourite of Queen Elizabeth I and apparently once laid his cloak across a muddy puddle so that she did not have to walk through it. Ralegh was also a poet, although most of his poems have been lost. He wrote poems as a way of discussing ideas with friends at the royal court. He formed a club known as 'The School of the Night' in order to discuss scientific discoveries and other subjects to do with the way the world was becoming more modern.

He had two sons, Wat and Carew, by his wife Bessie Throckmorton, and this poem is written for their benefit. The father is trying to warn a son that crimes can lead to capital punishment – which was legal in England in Tudor times. He also reminds them that their enemies could be out to frame them at any time.

After the death of Elizabeth I, King James I became monarch. He did not like Ralegh, accused him of plotting against the throne, and had his head cut off. His widow was presented with her husband's head, as tradition dictated, and she is said to have kept it beside her, at all times, concealed in a red leather bag.

MAYA ANGELOU
b. 1928

Still I Rise

You may write me down in history
With your bitter, twisted lies,
You may trod me in the very dirt
But still, like dust, I'll rise.

Does my sassiness upset you?
Why are you beset with gloom?
'Cause I walk like I've got oil wells
Pumping in my living room.

Just like moons and like suns,
With the certainty of tides,
Just like hopes springing high,
Still I'll rise.

Did you want to see me broken?
Bowed head and lowered eyes?
Shoulders falling down like teardrops,
Weakened by my soulful cries.

Does my haughtiness offend you?
Don't you take it awful hard
'Cause I laugh like I've got gold mines
Diggin' in my own back yard.

You may shoot me with your words,
You may cut me with your eyes,
You may kill me with your hatefulness,
But still, like air, I'll rise.

Does my sexiness upset you?
Does it come as a surprise
That I dance like I've got diamonds
At the meeting of my thighs?

Out of the huts of history's shame
I rise
Up from a past that's rooted in pain
I rise
I'm a black ocean, leaping and wide,
Welling and swelling I bear in the tide.

Leaving behind nights of terror and fear
I rise
Into a daybreak that's wondrously clear
I rise
Bringing the gifts that my ancestors gave,
I am the dream and the hope of the slave.
I rise
I rise
I rise.

Angelou was brought up in Missouri in the United States by her grandmother. She rarely saw her mother. She studied dancing and acting as a young woman and was a dedicated advocate for civil rights for black Americans. Her autobiography I Know Why the Caged Bird Sings, *became instantly famous and her poems talk about the struggles of the underclass. She never underestimates these struggles but always places her faith in the indomitable human spirit.*

LOUISE BENNETT
b. 1919

Colonization in Reverse

What a joyful news, Miss Mattie;
Ah feel like me heart gwine burs –
Jamaica people colonizin
England in reverse.

By de hundred, by de tousan,
From country an from town,
By de ship-load, by de plane-load.
Jamaica is Englan boun.

Dem a pour out a Jamaica;
Everybody future plan
Is fi get a big-time job
An settle in de motherlan.

What a islan! What a people!
Man an woman, ole an young
Jussa pack dem bag an baggage
An tun history upside dung!

Some people doan like travel,
But fi show dem loyalty
Dem all a open up cheap-fare-
To-Englan agency;

An week by week dem shippin off
Dem countryman like fire
Fi immigrate an populate
De seat a de Empire.

Oonoo se how life is funny,
Oonoo see de tunabout?
Jamaica live fi box bread
Out a English people mout.

For when dem catch a Englan
An start play dem different role
Some will settle down to work
An some will settle fi de dole.

Jane seh de dole is not too bad
Because dey payin she
Two pounds a week fi seek a job
Dat suit her dignity.

Me seh Jane will never fine work
At de rate how she dah look
For all day she stay pon Aunt Fan couch
An read love-story book.

What a devilment a Englan!
Dem face war an brave de worse;
But ah wonderin how dem gwine stan
Colonizin in reverse.

Louise Bennett was born in Kingston in Jamaica, in the West Indies. Her mother was a dressmaker and as a child 'Miss Lou', as she was known, noticed how her mother's clients enjoyed getting their dresses fitted. She also noticed though how uncomfortable they were when they talked in their black dialect — or patois. When she grew up Bennett put these experiences to work in her poetry: she employs a strong sense of comedy and uses the patois which was such a part of Jamaican life. It was an unusual thing for a Jamaican writer to do but, as Bennett said pointedly, why should she not use her own experiences rather than 'writing in the same old English way about autumn and things like that'.

MATTHEW SWEENEY
b. 1952

The Flying Spring Onion

The flying spring onion
flew through the air
over to where
the tomatoes grew in rows
and he said to those
seed-filled creatures
My rooted days are done,
so while you sit here
sucking sun
I'll be away and gone,
to Greenland
where they eat no green
and I won't be seen
in a salad bowl with you,
stung by lemon,
greased by oil,
and nothing at all to do
except wait to be eaten.
With that he twirled
his green propellers
and rose above the rows
of red balls
who stared as he grew small
and disappeared.

Sweeney was born in Donegal in Ireland, but has spent most of his adult life in London. He has published several collections of poems for young people and is a great believer in encouraging children in schools to read poetry.

40

PHAROAH AKHENATON
c. 1375 BC

Hymn to the Sun

A glory,
   eternity in life,
      the Undeposed,
   beauty
   flashing
   powers,

Love,
   the powering,
      the Widening,
      light
      unravelling
      all faces followers of

    All the colours, beams of
      woven thread,
        the Skin

      alight that
      warms itself
      with life.

    The Two Lands,
      shape themselves
        that Love

      flows
      to the
      making,

    Place, man, cattle, creature-kind,
      & tree of every image
        taking place.

Life-in-shining
shining
life,

The Mother/Father,
sees the Seeing
rise upon our

hearts beat
dawn lights
earth entire

As you made. And as you
pass we settle
equal to the Dead,

linen wrapping
head nostril
plugged with

Earth that waits
return in Heaven
rises overturned

the
uplift
palms upturned to

Light your being is
the living
Acts the

Touch the voicing in
all Land
hears Man –

Womansong en-
throning
Truth

gives
heart the
Food,

This One, we give, to walk,
purely to your
Will, all

creatures
dance you
toward your coming every

Day, you gave your
Son, forever in your
Form he

Acts
in
Beauty, saying:

I am
your Son, my heart
knows you the

strength
the seat
of powering

Eternal is the Light
you are the watchful
Maker,

solitary
every
life

Sees light that breathes
by light,
flowers

Seeding
Wilderness,
light stunned by

Light before your
Face,
the dancing

creatures,
feathers
up from nests a

Wavering in wing
goes round
around

& praises
          living
                    Joy

     you
     Are.

                         (trans. John Perlman)

WILLIAM SHAKESPEARE
1564-1616

Sonnet 106

When in the chronicle of wasted time
I see descriptions of the fairest wights,
And beauty making beautiful old rhyme
In praise of ladies dead and lovely knights,
Then, in the blazon of sweet beauty's best,
Of hand, of foot, of lip, of eye, of brow,
I see their antique pen would have express'd
Even such a beauty as you master now.
So all their praises are but prophecies
Of this our time, all you prefiguring;
And, for they look'd but with divining eyes,
They had not skill enough your worth to sing;
    For we, which now behold these present days,
    Have eyes to wonder, but lack tongues to praise.

This sonnet is rather like a riddle. It suggests that all the descriptions of beautiful things written in the past were a kind of prophecy of the beauty of the person to whom the sonnet is dedicated. The poet thinks that the person he is writing about is so beautiful that words cannot possibly capture the precise nature of that beauty.

T.S. ELIOT
1888–1965

Lines from The Waste Land

1. The Burial of the Dead
April is the cruellest month, breeding
Lilacs out of the dead land, mixing
Memory and desire, stirring
Dull roots with spring rain.
Winter kept us warm, covering
Earth in forgetful snow, feeding
A little life with dried tubers.

Summer surprised us, coming over the Starnbergersee
With a shower of rain; we stopped in the colonnade,
And went on in sunlight, into the Hofgarten,
And drank coffee, and talked for an hour.
Bin gar keine Russin, stamm' aus Litauen, echt deutsch.
And when we were children, staying at the archduke's,
My cousin's, he took me out on a sled,
And I was frightened. He said, Marie,
Marie, hold on tight. And down we went
In the mountains, there you feel free.
I read, much of the night, and go south in the winter.

Thomas Stearns Eliot was born in Missouri, in the United States, but emigrated to Britain and became a British citizen. He worked as a teacher and as Publishing Director of Faber & Faber, and is probably best remembered now as the author of Old Possums Book of Practical Cats *which was adapted as the musical,* Cats.

This poem reflects the uncertain and destructive era in which it was written. The characters in 'The Waste Land' do not welcome the spring. They are too disillusioned with life and prefer the barrenness of winter. Eliot began writing it in 1921 when there were many problems in Britain in the aftermath of the First World War: unemployment, an unstable economy and an indecisive government.

Ezra Pound helped him to edit the poem and once it was published many other young, aspiring poets tried to imitate its style.

e.e. cummings
1894–1962

what if a much of a which of a wind

what if a much of a which of a wind
gives the truth to summer's lie;
bloodies with dizzying leaves the sun
and yanks immortal stars awry?
Blow king to beggar and queen to seem
(blow friend to fiend: blow space to time)
– when skies are hanged and oceans drowned,
the single secret will still be man

what if a keen of a lean wind flays
screaming hills with sleet and snow;
strangles valleys by ropes of thing
and stifles forests in white ago?
Blow hope to terror; blow seeing to blind
(blow pity to envy and soul to mind)
– whose hearts are mountains, roots are trees,
it's they shall cry hello to the spring

what if a dawn of a doom of a dream
bites this universe in two,
peels forever out of his grave
and sprinkles nowhere with me and you?
Blow soon to never and never to twice
(blow life to isn't: blow death to was)
– all nothing's only our hugest home;
the most who die, the more we live

Cummings was born in Massachusetts, in the United States. As a child he loved books, and even had a study in his tree house in the back garden. Later Cummings's writing began to imitate the jazz music and cubist style of painting fashionable at that time. He was fascinated by the way cubist painters broke up familiar shapes in their paintings and he tried to break up and mingle words on the page in the same way. He also mimicked the irregular tone of jazz in the way he brought words together.

RUPERT BROOKE
1887–1915

The Soldier

If I should die, think only this of me;
  That there's some corner of a foreign field
That is for ever England. There shall be
  In that rich earth a richer dust concealed;
A dust whom England bore, shaped, made aware,
  Gave, once, her flowers to love, her ways to roam,
A body of England's breathing English air,
  Washed by the rivers, blest by suns of home.

And think, this heart, all evil shed away,
  A pulse in the eternal mind, no less
    Gives somewhere back the thoughts by England given;
Her sights and sounds; dreams happy as her day;
  And laughter, learnt of friends; and gentleness,
    In hearts at peace, under an English heaven.

———

Brooke died of blood poisoning on his way to Gallipoli in 1915. This was only one year into the senseless horrors of the First World War and the anger about the sacrifice and suffering of so many young men were yet to make their mark on poetry written by fighting men. Looked at today, Brooke's war poetry comes across as unquestioning and patriotic when set against the brutal honesty of Wilfred Owen, Siegfried Sassoon or Robert Graves.

50

BENJAMIN ZEPHANIAH
b. 1958

Derek in Heaven

Derek in heaven
Swallowed a poem
That little poem
Just kept on growing,
Derek grew bigger
Until she was big
Then Derek the beetle
Turned into a pig.
This pig could fly
Well that's what I heard
Then our heavenly piggy
Turned into a bird,
Bird brainy Derek
Loved flying around
In this animal heaven
Where poems are found.
What's more amazing
Is that in her youth
Bird brainy Derek
Turned into a fruit,
Derek got ripe
Derek stood proud
And this juicy fruity
Would shout very loud,
This musical fruit
Had a wonderful habit
Of rapping
So then she turned into a rabbit,
One day she went into
God's great big hat
And what did she do,
She turned into a rat.
This cool rat rapper
Had the eyes of an eagle
One day as she rapped
She turned into a beetle,

Then Derek the beetle
Found heaven's big tree,
There she thrives on a diet
Of pure poetry.

The name Benjamin Zephaniah is now very well known in England. Zephaniah was born in Jamaica but came to live in England when he was two years old. His poems are invariably humorous but the messages they convey are serious. He is passionate about justice and equality. Expelled from school as a child, he was sent to Borstal, but as he grew older he became involved with performance poetry and music as a way of giving vent to his frustrations and expressing his own opinions. His poems have a marvellous rythym.

He is the only Rastafarian poet ever to have been nominated for the position of Professor of Poetry at Oxford University (1988). He lost to Seamus Heaney.

WILLIAM WORDSWORTH
1770–1850

The Solitary Reaper

Behold her, single in the field,
Yon solitary Highland Lass!
Reaping and singing by herself;
Stop here, or gently pass!
Alone she cuts and binds the grain,
And sings a melancholy strain;
O listen! for the Vale profound
Is overflowing with the sound.

No Nightingale did ever chaunt
More welcome notes to weary bands
Of travellers in some shady haunt,
Among Arabian sands;
A voice so thrilling ne'er was heard
In springtime from the Cuckoo bird,
Breaking the silence of the seas
Among the farthest Hebrides.

Will no one tell me what she sings? –
Perhaps the plaintive numbers flow
For old, unhappy, far-off things.
And battles long ago;
Or is it some more humble lay,
Familiar matter of today?
Some natural sorrow, loss, or pain,
That has been, and may be again?

Whate'er the theme, the Maiden sang
As if her song could have no ending;
I saw her singing at her work,
And o'er the sickle bending –
I listened, motionless and still;
And, as I mounted up the hill,
The music in my heart I bore,
Long after it was heard no more.

OGDEN NASH
1902–1971

The Cow

The cow is of the bovine ilk;
One end is moo, the other, milk.

WALT WHITMAN
1819–1892

O Captain! My Captain!

O Captain! my Captain! our fearful trip is done,
The ship has weathered every rack, the prize we sought is won,
The port is near, the bells I hear, the people all exulting,
While follow eyes the steady keel, the vessel grim and daring;
    But O heart! heart! heart!
      O the bleeding drops of red!
        Where on the deck my Captain lies,
          Fallen cold and dead.

O Captain! my Captain! rise up and hear the bells;
Rise up – for you the flag is flung – for you the bugle trills,
For you bouquets and ribboned wreaths – for you the shores a-crowding,
For you they call, the swaying mass, their eager faces turning;
    Here, Captain! dear father!
      This arm beneath your head!
        It is some dream that on the deck
          You've fallen cold and dead.

My Captain does not answer, his lips are pale and still,
My father does not feel my arm, he has no pulse nor will;
The ship is anchored safe and sound, its voyage closed and done,
From fearful trip the victor ship comes in with object won;
    Exult, O shores! and ring, O bells!
      But I, with mournful tread,
        Walk the deck my Captain lies,
          Fallen cold and dead.

Whitman was one of the first American poets to achieve an international reputation. He had various jobs. He was a speech writer, printer, journalist and a volunteer nurse in the American Civil War. He was keen to promote democratic ideas and had a real concern for equality. He also liked bus rides and stylish clothes. His poetry established 'free verse' and encouraged writers to use unconventional rhythms and not to worry too much about rhyme.

ROBERT BURNS
1759–1796

A Red, Red Rose

O my luve's like a red, red rose,
    That's newly sprung in June;
O my luve's like the melodie
    That's sweetly played in tune.

As fair art thou, my bonnie lass,
    So deep in luve am I;
And I will luve thee still, my dear,
    Till a' the seas gang dry.

Till a' the seas gang dry, my dear,
    And the rocks melt wi' the sun:
O I will love thee still, my dear,
    While the sands o' life shall run.

And fare thee weel, my only luve,
    And fare thee weel awhile!
And I will come again, my luve,
    Though it were ten thousand mile.

Burns grew up working as a labourer on his father's farm in Scotland. As a teenager he enjoyed debating and dancing. His father did not approve. His first poem 'Handsome Nell' was said to have been written at the age of seventeen for a young girl with whom he worked in the fields. Burns usually wrote in Scottish dialect which he learnt travelling around Scotland, listening to and writing down traditional songs and ballads.

Poems such as 'A Red, Red Rose' were composed like mosaics. The words and phrases were not original but were borrowed from popular old Scottish songs. Burns had a sharp ear for conversational language and he created powerful poems echoing the stories families passed on through the generations.

IBARAGI NORIKO
b. 1926

What a Little Girl had on her Mind

What a little girl had on her mind was:
Why do the shoulders of other men's wives
give off so strong a smell like magnolia;
or like gardenias?
What is it,
that faint veil of mist,
over the shoulders of other men's wives?
She wanted to have one,
that wonderful thing
even the prettiest virgin cannot have.

The little girl grew up.
She became a wife and then a mother.
One day she suddenly realized;
the tenderness
that gathers over the shoulders of wives,
is only fatigue
from loving others day after day.

(trans. Kenneth Rexroth and Ikuko Atsumi)

T.S. ELIOT
1888–1965

Lines from Little Gidding

I

Midwinter spring is its own season
Sempiternal though sodden towards sundown,
Suspended in time, between pole and tropic.
When the short day is brightest, with frost and fire,
The brief sun flames the ice, on pond and ditches,
In windless cold that is the heart's heat,
Reflecting in a watery mirror
A glare that is blindness in the early afternoon.
And glow more intense than blaze of branch, or brazier,
Stirs the dumb spirit: no wind, but pentecostal fire
In the dark time of the year. Between melting and freezing
The soul's sap quivers. There is no earth smell
Or smell of living thing. This is the spring time
But not in time's covenant. Now the hedgerow
Is blanched for an hour with transitory blossom
Of snow, a bloom more sudden
Than that of summer, neither budding nor fading,
Not in the scheme of generation.
Where is the summer, the unimaginable
Zero summer?

———————————

Little Gidding, in Huntingdonshire, is the site of an Anglican religious community which was run by Nicholas Ferrar from 1626 to 1646. The community was concerned with giving help to the poor and needy but it was eventually disbanded by Cromwell's Puritan army. It was remembered as an example of Christian communal living and it inspired this poem, one of TS Eliot's 'Four Quartets'.

PERCY BYSSHE SHELLEY
1792–1822

To———

Music, when soft voices die,
Vibrates in the memory –
Odours, when sweet violets sicken,
Live within the sense they quicken.
Rose leaves, when the rose is dead,
Are heaped for the belovéd's bed,
And so my thoughts, when thou art gone,
Love itself shall slumber on.

Shelley had passionate ideas about reforming the world. He was expelled from Oxford University for publishing a pamphlet entitled 'The Necessity of Atheism' at a time when the university was strongly associated with the Church of England. He was interested in philosophy, morality and politics. Like his close friend Byron he loved the sea, but he could not swim and drowned when his boat capsized. His wife, Mary Shelley, was the author of the original Frankenstein story.

CHARLES BUKOWSKI
1920–1994

the trash men

here they come
these guys
gray truck
radio playing

they are in a hurry

it's quite exciting:
shirt open
bellies hanging out

they run out the trash bins
roll them out to the fork lift
and then the truck grinds it upward
with far too much sound . . .

they had to fill out application forms
to get these jobs
they are paying for homes and
drive late model cars

they get drunk on Saturday night

now in the Los Angeles sunshine
they run back and forth with their trash bins

all that trash goes somewhere

and they shout to each other

then they are all up in the truck
driving west toward the sea

none of them know
that I am alive

REX DISPOSAL CO.

Charles Bukowski is famous for his bad boy image. His poetry is autobiographical and deals with life as a poor man in Los Angeles – observations of city life, getting into fights and wondering how he will pay for his next bottle of whisky. Bukowski loved city life – 'blaring car horns and dirty sidewalks' made him feel at home, he said.

WILLIAM WORDSWORTH
1770–1850

The Daffodils

I wandered lonely as a cloud
That floats on high o'er vales and hills,
When all at once I saw a crowd,
A host of golden daffodils,
Beside the lake, beneath the trees,
Fluttering and dancing in the breeze.

Continuous as the stars that shine
And twinkle on the milky way,
They stretched in never-ending line
Along the margin of a bay:
Ten thousand saw I at a glance
Tossing their heads in sprightly dance.

The waves beside them danced, but they
Out-did the sparkling waves in glee:
A poet could not but be gay
In such a jocund company!
I gazed – and gazed – but little thought
What wealth the show to me had brought.

For oft, when on my couch I lie
In vacant or in pensive mood,
They flash upon that inward eye
Which is the bliss of solitude;
And then my heart with pleasure fills,
And dances with the daffodils.

––––––––

The poet explains how the beauty of this array of flowers in their natural setting comes back to him at unexpected moments. The picture of the daffodils brings him comfort, and he reminds us that even when we are lonely, surprise encounters can be a delight.

GWENDOLYN BROOKS
b. 1917

We Real Cool

The Pool Players.
Seven at the Golden Shovel.

We real cool. We
Left school. We

Lurk late. We
Strike straight. We

Sing sin. We
Thin gin. We

Jazz June. We
Die soon.

WILLIAM SHAKESPEARE
1564-1616

Lines from *The Tempest*

Cal. Be not afeard. The Isle is full of noises,
Sounds, and sweet airs, that give delight, and hurt not.
Sometimes a thousand twangling instruments
Will hum about mine ears; and sometime voices,
That, if I then had wak'd after long sleep,
Will make me sleep again; and then, in dreaming,
The clouds methought would open and show riches
Ready to drop upon me, that, when I wak'd,
I cried to dream again.

This is a speech from Shakespeare's play, The Tempest. *Caliban is a rebellious character, half-fish and half-human. He is described in the play as a 'savage and deformed slave'. The magician, Prospero, dislikes Caliban and is forever insulting him, but in this speech Caliban shows his human sensitivity. He wants to escape the mocking and ridicule. His words remind us that dreams and music can have the power to make us feel hopeful about life, despite its many problems.*

OLIVER GOLDSMITH
1730–1774

When Lovely Woman Stoops to Folly

When lovely woman stoops to folly,
  And finds too late that men betray,
What charm can soothe her melancholy,
  What art can wash her guilt away?

The only art her guilt to cover,
  To hide her shame from every eye,
To give repentance to her lover,
  And wring his bosom – is to die.

---

*Goldsmith was a brilliant and prolific Irish poet and playwright. His play,
She Stoops to Conquer, first produced in 1773, was extremely successful.
It's about peoples' greed for wealth and status and how that affects
relationships. The short poem tells the story of a woman seeking a
commitment from a man, only to realize she has a more romantic view of
her love affair than he does.*

ERIC ROACH
1915–1974

At Guaracara Park

the bronze god running,
beauty hurtling through the web of air,
motion fusing time and space
exploding our applauses . . .

speed was survival there in the green heat
where the lithe hero dashed
from the leopard's leap,
fled to cover from the feral fang
or ran the antelope across the plains.

and speed and stamina were the warrior's pride
where impis of assegais and swords and shields
tore tigerish through the brush and raided
and bounced back upon the kraals
panting from wounds and weariness,
brandishing the trophies of their cradling war.
the slave ships could not break our bones
nor strip our tendons, nor the long slaving
years narrow our arteries nor disease
our lungs nor shrivel up our hearts,
but left love thundering to this running man.

not fame's wreath crowns him
but Ogun's aura now; that blaze of flame
that savaged history back beyond our memories
our dreams and searchings.
the blood of the fierce gods we lost,
the pantheon of the kraals made him immortal
or he would have been a scarecrow in the canes.

OGDEN NASH
1902–1971

Requiem

There was a young belle of old Natchez
Whose garments were always in patchez.
When comment arose
On the state of her clothes,
She drawled, When Ah itchez, Ah scratchez!

CHARLES KINGSLEY
1819–1875

The Sands of Dee

'O Mary, go and call the cattle home,
    And call the cattle home,
    And call the cattle home
  Across the sands of Dee;'
The western wind was wild and dank with foam,
  And all alone went she.

The western tide crept up along the sand,
    And o'er and o'er the sand,
    And round and round the sand,
  As far as eye could see.
The rolling mist came down and hid the land:
  And never home came she.

'Oh! is it weed, or fish, or floating hair –
    A tress of golden hair,
    A drownéd maiden's hair
  Above the nets at sea?
Was never salmon yet that shone so fair
  Among the stakes on Dee.'

They rowed her in across the rolling foam,
    The cruel crawling foam,
    The cruel hungry foam,
  To her grave beside the sea:
But still the boatmen hear her call the cattle home
  Across the sands of Dee.

Kingsley worked as a rector and was a founder member of the Christian Socialist movement. He is best remembered for his famous children's story, The Water Babies. *He wanted, in his writing, to encourage tolerance and to shock his readers into recognizing the cruel effects of poverty on people's lives.*

BEN JONSON
1572–1637

Song: to Celia

Drink to me only with thine eyes,
And I will pledge with mine;
Or leave a kiss but in the cup,
And I'll not look for wine.
The thirst that from the soul doth rise,
Doth ask a drink divine:
But might I of Jove's nectar sup,
I would not change for thine.

I sent thee late a rosy wreath,
Not so much honouring thee,
As giving it a hope, that there
It could not withered be.
But thou thereon did'st only breathe,
And sent'st it back to me;
Since when it grows and smells, I swear,
Not of itself, but thee.

Ben Jonson's first job was as a bricklayer, working for his stepfather. It was not a profession he enjoyed. By his mid-twenties he was working as an actor and a playwright. His most famous play, Everyman in his Humour, *had* William Shakespeare *acting in the cast when it was first performed. Jonson was known as an aggressive and provocative man, but his poems – particularly those dedicated to this children, who died very young – show great tenderness and humanity.*

WILLIAM WORDSWORTH
1770–1850

Elegiac Stanzas

I was thy neighbor once, thou rugged Pile!
Four summer weeks I dwelt in sight of thee:
I saw thee every day; and all the while
Thy Form was sleeping on a glassy sea.

So pure the sky, so quiet was the air!
So like, so very like, was day to day!
Whene'er I looked, thy Image still was there;
It trembled, but it never passed away.

How perfect was the calm! it seemed no sleep;
No mood, which season takes away, or brings:
I could have fancied that the mighty Deep
Was even the gentlest of all gentle Things.

Ah! THEN, if mine had been the Painter's hand,
To express what then I saw; and add the gleam,
The light that never was, on sea or land,
The consecration, and the Poet's dream;

I would have planted thee, thou hoary Pile
Amid a world how different from this!
Beside a sea that could not cease to smile;
On tranquil land, beneath a sky of bliss.

Thou shouldst have seemed a treasure house divine
O peaceful years; a chronicle of heaven—
Of all the sunbeams that did ever shine
The very sweetest had to thee been given.

A Picture had it been of lasting ease,
Elysian quiet, without toil or strife;
No motion but the moving tide, a breeze,
Or merely silent Nature's breathing life.

Such, in the fond illusion of my heart,
Such Picture would I at that time have made,
And seen the soul of truth in every part
A steadfast peace that might not betrayed.

So once it would have been – 'tis so no more;
I have submitted to a new control:
A power is gone, which nothing can restore;
A deep distress hath humanized my Soul

DEREK WALCOTT
b. 1930

Islands

Merely to name them is the prose
Of diarists, to make you a name
For readers who like travellers praise
Their beds and beaches as the same;
But islands can only exist
If we have loved in them. I seek,
As climate seeks its style, to write
Verse crisp as sand, clear as sunlight,
Cold as the curled wave, ordinary
As a tumbler of island water;
Yet, like a diarist, thereafter
I savour their salt-haunted rooms
(Your body stirring the creased sea
Of crumpled sheets), whose mirrors lose
Our huddled, sleeping images,
Like words which love had hoped to use
Erased with the surf's pages.

So, like a diarist in sand,
I mark the peace with which you graced
Particular islands, descending
A narrow stair to light the lamps
Against the night surf's noises, shielding
A leaping mantle with one hand,
Or simply scaling fish for supper,
Onions, jack-fish, bread, red snapper;
And on each kiss the harsh sea-taste,
And how by moonlight you were made
To study most the surf's unyielding
Patience though it seems a waste.

Walcott was born in St Lucia, in the West Indies, and one of the main
themes in his poetry is the idea of rootlessness — the rootlessness of the
diaspora, of the feeling that you don't belong or fit in with any one culture

or race. Some of his poems use the Creole Patois dialect that is still spoken in St Lucia, but his writing always fixes strong visual images in the reader's mind. Walcott, who has won the Nobel Prize for Literature, is also a painter and is fascinated by the relationship between words and images.

PERCY BYSSHE SHELLEY
1792–1822

Ozymandias

I met a traveller from an antique land
Who said: Two vast and trunkless legs of stone
Stand in the desert . . . Near them, on the sand,
Half sunk, a shattered visage lies, whose frown,
And wrinkled lip, and sneer of cold command,
Tell that its sculptor well those passions read
Which yet survive, stamped on these lifeless things,
The hand that mocked them, and the heart that fed:
And on the pedestal these words appear:
'My name is Ozymandias, king of kings:
Look on my works, ye Mighty, and despair!'
Nothing beside remains. Round the decay
Of that colossal wreck, boundless and bare
The lone and level sands stretch far away.

This poem takes the subject of an Egyptian king buried, as tradition dictated, with his possessions. Shelley implies that mere possessions can never bring immortality and however famous we might be, our name can still be forgotten.

MITSUHARU KANEKO
1895–1975

Mount Fuji

Like the inside of a picnic box
Japan is tiny and self-contained

From corner to corner, with scrupulous care,
We are all counted, one by one,

so that we get called up to fight in the forces
in a most disgraceful way.

Census register book, be burned to ashes
so that no one may remember my son.

My son,
come here and hide away between my hands,
come and hide underneath my hat for a little while.

Your father and mother, in the inn at the mountain foot,
discussed the matter all night long.

Rain was falling all night long,
drenching the naked trees,
with the sounds of breaking twigs.

My son, drenched to the skin,
dragging a heavy rifle, gasping for breath,
I see you tramping along in a daze.
Where are you, my son?

Not knowing where you are,
your father and mother go wandering to look for you
in a night-long dream that lasts until
daybreak brings to an end the long, disturbed night.

We wake to see the rain is over, but
not our nightmare. And in a vacant sky,
dull as damnation, like some
shabby old bathrobe faded in the wash,
— Mount Fuji

(trans. James Kirkup and Akiko Takemoto)

CHRISTINA ROSSETTI
1830–1894

Up-Hill

Does the road wind up-hill all the way?
  Yes, to the very end.
Will the day's journey take the whole long day?
  From morn to night, my friend.

But is there for the night a resting-place?
  A roof for when the slow dark hours begin.
May not the darkness hide it from my face?
  You cannot miss that inn.

Shall I meet other wayfarers at night?
  Those who have gone before.
Then must I knock, or call when just in sight?
  They will not keep you standing at that door.

Shall I find comfort, travel-sore and weak?
  Of labour you shall find the sum.
Will there be beds for me and all who seek?
  Yea, beds for all who come.

_____

The sister of the Pre-Raphaelite painter Dante Gabriel Rossetti, Christina was a committed Christian. While her brother was out at parties or fussing over girlfriends, Christina stayed at home to look after their mother. Her poems focus on the struggles surrounding her faith in God. She turned down two proposals of marriage because the men in question did not share her High Anglican Christian beliefs.

SAMUEL TAYLOR COLERIDGE
1772–1834

The Rime of the Ancient Mariner

Part I

It is an ancient Mariner
And he stoppeth one of three.
– 'By thy long gray beard and glittering eye,
Now wherefore stopp'st thou me?

The Bridegroom's doors are opened wide,
And I am next of kin;
The guests are met, the feast is set:
May'st hear the merry din.'

He holds him with his skinny hand,
'There was a ship,' quoth he,
'Hold off! unhand me, graybeard loon!'
Eftsoons his hand dropped he.

He holds him with his glittering eye –
The Wedding Guest stood still,
And listens like a three years' child:
The Mariner hath his will.

The Wedding Guest sat on a stone:
He cannot choose but hear;
And thus spake on that ancient man,
The bright-eyed Mariner.

'The ship was cheered, the harbor cleared,
Merrily did we drop
Below the kirk, below the hill,
Below the lighthouse top.

The Sun came up upon the left,
Out of the sea came he!
And he shone bright, and on the right
Went down into the sea.

Higher and higher every day,
Till over the mast at noon –'
The Wedding Guest here beat his breast,
For he heard the loud bassoon.

The bride hath paced into the hall,
Red as a rose is she;
Nodding their heads before her goes
The merry minstrelsy.

The Wedding Guest he beat his breast,
Yet he cannot choose but hear;
And thus spake on that ancient man,
The bright-eyed Mariner.

'And now the STORM-BLAST came, and he
Was tyrannous and strong;
He struck with his o'ertaking wings,
And chased us south along.

With sloping masts and dipping prow,
As who pursued with yell and blow
Still treads the shadow of his foe,
And forward bends his head,
The ship drove fast, loud roared the blast,
And southward aye we fled.

And now there came both mist and snow,
And it grew wondrous cold:
And ice, mast-high, came floating by,
As green as emerald.

And through the drifts the snowy clifts
Did send a dismal sheen:
Nor shapes of men nor beasts we ken –
The ice was all between.

The ice was here, the ice was there,
The ice was all around:
It cracked and growled, and roared and howled,
Like noises in a swound!

At length did cross an Albatross,
Thorough the fog it came;
As if it had been a Christian soul,
We hailed it in God's name.

It ate the food it ne'er had eat,
And round and round it flew.
The ice did split with a thunder-fit;
The helmsman steered us through!

And a good south wind sprung up behind;
The Albatross did follow,
And every day, for food or play,
Came to the mariners' hollo!

In mist or cloud, on mast or shroud,
It perched for vespers nine;
Whiles all the night, through fog-smoke white,
Glimmered the white Moon-shine.'

'God save thee, ancient Mariner!
From the fiends, that plague thee thus! –
Why look'st thou so?' – With my crossbow
I shot the ALBATROSS.

Coleridge, who was born in Devon, acquired a great interest in people's behaviour and beliefs, so much so that the poet Shelley once called him 'a subtle-souled psychologist'. Like his friend Wordsworth, Coleridge was also concerned about our relationship with the natural world.

This mysterious, magical poem tells of a sailor who shoots an albatross and upsets the spirit of nature. As a punishment the sailor is forced to wander all over the world for the rest of his life. He loses his ship, and is cursed with retelling his story endlessly.

JOHN DRYDEN
1631–1700

Happy the Man

Happy the man and happy he alone,
   He who can call today his own:
   He who, secure within, can say,
Tomorrow do thy worst, for I have lived today.
   Be fair or foul or rain or shine
The joys I have possessed, in spite of fate, are mine.
Not Heaven itself upon the past has power,
But what has been, has been, and I have had my hour.

Dryden had a great influence on the writing style of the seventeenth century. He was known to friends, such as Alexander Pope, as 'Glorious John'. He enjoyed meeting other writers at Will's Coffee House in London. In this poem Dryden emphasizes the need to draw strength from all life's experience. He asserts that no one can take our history away, and that it can always help us to face life's hurdles.

GUILLAUME APOLLINAIRE
(William Apollineris de Kostrowitski)
1880–1918

Mirabeau Bridge

Under the Mirabeau Bridge there flows the Seine
    Must I recall
  Our loves recall how then
After each sorrow joy came back again

    Let night come on bells end the day
    The days go by me still I stay

Hands joined and face to face let's stay just so
    While underneath
The bridge of our arms shall go
Weary of endless looks the river's flow

    Let night come on bells end the day
    The days go by me still I stay

All love goes by as water to the sea
    All love goes by
How slow life seems to me
How violent the hope of love can be

    Let night come on bells end the day
    The days go by me still I stay

The days the weeks pass by beyond our ken
    Neither time past
Nor love comes back again
Under the Mirabeau Bridge there flows the Seine

    Let night come on bells end the day
    The days go by me still I stay

(trans. Richard Wilbur)

ALFRED, LORD TENNYSON
1809–1892

The Charge of the Light Brigade

Half a league, half a league,
  Half a league onward,
All in the valley of Death
  Rode the six hundred.
'Forward, the Light Brigade!
Charge for the guns!' he said:
Into the valley of Death
  Rode the six hundred.

'Forward, the Light Brigade!'
Was there a man dismay'd?
Not tho' the soldier knew
  Some one had blunder'd:
Their's not to make reply,
Their's not to reason why,
Their's but to do and die:
Into the valley of Death
  Rode the six hundred.

Cannon to right of them,
Cannon to left of them,
Cannon in front of them
  Volley'd and thunder'd;
Storm'd at with shot and shell,
Boldly they rode and well,
Into the jaws of Death,
Into the mouth of Hell
  Rode the six hundred.

Flash'd all their sabres bare,
Flash'd as they turn'd in air
Sabring the gunners there,
Charging an army, while
    All the world wonder'd:
Plunged in the battery smoke
Right thro' the line they broke;
Cossack and Russian
Reel'd from the sabre-stroke
    Shatter'd and sunder'd.
Then they rode back, but not
    Not the six hundred.

Cannon to right of them,
Cannon to left of them,
Cannon behind them
    Volley'd and thunder'd;
Storm'd at with shot and shell,
While horse and hero fell,
They that had fought so well
Came thro' the jaws of Death,
Back from the mouth of Hell,
All that was left of them,
    Left of six hundred.

When can their glory fade?
O the wild charge they made!
    All the world wonder'd.
Honour the charge they made!
Honour the Light Brigade,
    Noble six hundred!

———————————————

This is a poem about the Crimean War, and it was written on 2 December 1854 after Tennyson read a report about it in The Times *newspaper. He was inspired by the phrase 'Someone has blundered'. Reading this poem aloud helps us appreciate its persuasive rhythm – a sense of soldiers galloping on horses.*

EDWARD LEAR
1813–1888

There Was an Old Man with a Beard

There was an Old Man with a beard,
Who said, 'It is just as I feared! –
Two Owls and a Hen, four Larks and a Wren,
Have all built their nests in my beard!'

Lear was a writer and an artist who travelled extensively. He loved painting landscapes but he also had a job painting pictures of animals in London's zoological gardens. He was always short of money so he encouraged rich friends to buy his paintings and soon discovered that they liked his sense of humour and his ability to make up daft and improbable stories. His Book of Nonsense *was written for the grandchildren of his patron, the Earl of Derby.*

CHRISTINA ROSSETTI
1830–1894

Remember

Remember me when I am gone away,
   Gone far away into the silent land;
   When you can no more hold me by the hand,
Nor I half turn to go yet turning stay.
Remember me when no more day by day
   You tell me of our future that you planned:
   Only remember me; you understand
It will be late to counsel then or pray.
Yet if you should forget me for a while
   And afterwards remember, do not grieve:
   For if the darkness and corruption leave
   A vestige, of the thoughts that once I had,
Better by far you should forget and smile
   Than that you should remember and be sad.

R.S. THOMAS
b.1913

Gifts

From my father my strong heart,
My weak stomach.
From my mother the fear.

From my sad country the shame.

To my wife all I have
Saving only the love
That is not mine to give.

To my one son the hunger.

Thomas was a vicar in rural Wales for much of his life, and he was very preoccupied with the problems of the farmers and their families. He saw how hard they had to work to earn a living. Most of his poems are about keeping faith in God even when the world around us seems harsh and cruel.

RAYMOND CARVER
1939–1988

Happiness

So early it's still almost dark out.
I'm near the window with coffee,
and the usual early morning stuff
that passes for thought.
When I see the boy and his friend
walking up the road
to deliver the newspaper.
They wear caps and sweaters,
and one boy has a bag over his shoulder.
They are so happy
they aren't saying anything, these boys.
I think if they could, they would take
each other's arm.
It's early in the morning,
and they are doing this thing together.
They come on, slowly.
The sky is taking on light,
though the moon still hangs pale over the water.
Such beauty that for a minute
death and ambition, even love,
doesn't enter into this.
Happiness. It comes on
unexpectedly. And goes beyond, really,
any early morning talk about it.

Raymond Carver was a renowned American poet and short story writer.
He wrote in a clear, unfussy style, and quite often about the sad and
complicated situations we are called upon to deal with. As a young man
he was too busy working to support his family to have much time to write,
but when his marriage broke up and he gave up drink he devoted his time
to writing.

In this poem he has some sentimental recollections about the freedom of being a young boy with his first job. He doesn't focus on all the miserable things about doing a paper round, like being stuck out in the rain. Instead he reminds the reader of the importance of friendship and understanding between two people.

JOHN KEATS
1795–1821

When I Have Fears

When I have fears that I may cease to be
  Before my pen has gleaned my teeming brain,
Before high-piléd books, in charact'ry,
  Hold like rich garners the full-ripened grain;
When I behold, upon the night's starred face,
  Huge cloudy symbols of a high romance,
And think that I may never live to trace
  Their shadows, with the magic hand of chance;
And when I feel, fair creature of an hour,
  That I shall never look upon thee more,
Never have relish in the faery power
  Of unreflecting love! – then on the shore
Of the wide world I stand alone, and think
Till Love and Fame to nothingness do sink.

Keats was born in London and as a young man studied medicine, but he gave up the prospect of becoming a doctor to concentrate on his writing. He admired the poetry of Shakespeare and Milton. Fanny Burney, one of his Hampstead neighbours, captured his affections, but their relationship was cut short when Keats became ill with consumption and died in Rome at the age of only twenty-six.

This poem was written in January 1818. It's inspired by Shakespeare's sonnets and focuses on similar concerns about love, poetic ambition and the passing of time.

JOHN CLARE
1793–1864

I Am

I am: yet what I am none cares or knows
  My friends forsake me like a memory lost,
I am the self-consumer of my woes –
  They rise and vanish in oblivious host,
Like shadows in love's frenzied, stifled throes –
  And yet I am, and live – like vapours tossed

Into the nothingness of scorn and noise,
  Into the living sea of waking dreams,
Where there is neither sense of life or joys,
  But the vast shipwreck of my life's esteems;
Even the dearest, that I love the best,
Are strange – nay, rather stranger than the rest.

I long for scenes, where man hath never trod,
  A place where woman never smiled or wept –
There to abide with my Creator, God,
  And sleep as I in childhood sweetly slept,
Untroubling, and untroubled where I lie,
The grass below – above the vaulted sky.

———————

John Clare grew up in a farming community with parents who both liked songs and storytelling. As an adult he worked as a farm labourer and gardener and had eight children of his own. There was always a struggle to make ends meet and the strain of supporting his family contributed to a nervous breakdown. He spent most of the last twenty-seven years of his life in asylums suffering from delusions. It was reported that he sometimes thought he was the successful poet, Lord Byron; other times he thought he was Jack Randall, a boxer.

T.S. ELIOT
1888–1965

Macavity: the Mystery Cat

Macavity's a Mystery Cat: he's called the Hidden Paw –
For he's the master criminal who can defy the Law.
He's the bafflement of Scotland Yard, the Flying Squad's despair:
For when they reach the scene of crime – *Macavity's not there!*

Macavity, Macavity, there's no one like Macavity,
He's broken every human law, he breaks the law of gravity.
His powers of levitation would make a fakir stare,
And when you reach the scene of crime – *Macavity's not there!*
You may seek him in the basement, you may look up in the air –
But I tell you once and once again, *Macavity's not there!*

Macavity's a ginger cat, he's very tall and thin;
You would know him if you saw him, for his eyes are sunken in.
His brow is deeply lined with thought, his head is highly domed;
His coat is dusty from neglect, his whiskers are uncombed.
He sways his head from side to side, with movements like a snake;
And when you think he's half asleep, he's always wide awake.

Macavity, Macavity, there's no one like Macavity,
For he's a fiend in feline shape, a monster of depravity.
You may meet him in a by-street, you may see him in the square –
But when a crime's discovered, then *Macavity's not there!*

He's outwardly respectable. (They say he cheats at cards.)
And his footprints are not found in any file of Scotland Yard's.
And when the larder's looted, or thejewel-case is rifled,
Or when the milk is missing, or another Peke's been stifled,
Or the greenhouse glass is broken, and the trellis past repair –
Ay, there's the wonder of the thing! *Macavity's not there!*

And when the Foreign Office find a Treaty's gone astray,
Or the Admiralty lose some plans and drawings by the way,
There may be a scrap of paper in the hall or on the stair –
But it's useless to investigate – *Macavity's not there!*
And when the loss has been disclosed, the Secret Service say:
'It *must* have been Macavity!' – but he's a mile away.
You'll be sure to find him resting, or a-licking of his thumbs,
Or engaged in doing complicated long division sums.

Macavity, Macavity, there's no one like Macavity,
There never was a Cat of such deceitfulness and suavity.
He always has an alibi, and one or two to spare:
At whatever time the deed took place – MACAVITY WASN'T THERE!
And they say that all the Cats whose wicked deeds are widely
    known
(I might mention Mungojerrie, I might mention Griddlebone)
Are nothing more than agents for the Cat who all the time
Just controls their operations: the Napoleon of Crime!

WILLIAM BUTLER YEATS
1865–1939

The Lake Isle of Innisfree

I will arise and go now, and go to Innisfree,
And a small cabin build there, of clay and wattles made:
Nine bean-rows will I have there, a hive for the honey-bee,
And live alone in the bee-loud glade.

And I shall have some peace there, for peace comes dropping slow,
Dropping from the veils of the morning to where the cricket sings;
There midnight's all a glimmer, and noon a purple glow,
And evening full of the linnet's wings.

I will arise and go now, for always night and day
I hear lake water lapping with low sounds by the shore;
While I stand on the roadway, or on the pavements grey,
I hear it in the deep heart's core.

When Yeats lived in London he was frequently homesick for Sligo in Ireland, where he had lived when he was young. This poem shows his longing for simplicity. It was inspired by a small fountain which caught his eye in a shop window and made him think of the countryside.

LEWIS CARROLL
1832–1898

Father William

'You are old, Father William,' the young man said,
   'And your hair has become very white;
And yet you incessantly stand on your head –
   Do you think, at your age, it is right?'

'In my youth,' Father William replied to his son,
   'I feared it might injure the brain;
But, now that I'm perfectly sure I have none,
   Why, I do it again and again.'

'You are old,' said the youth, 'as I mentioned before,
   And have grown most uncommonly fat;
Yet you turned a back-somersault in at the door –
   Pray, what is the reason of that?'

'In my youth,' said the sage, as he shook his grey locks,
   'I kept all my limbs very supple
By the use of this ointment – one shilling the box –
   Allow me to sell you a couple?'

'You are old,' said the youth, 'and your jaws are too weak
   For anything tougher than suet;
Yet you finished the goose, with the bones and the beak –
   Pray, how did you manage to do it?'

'In my youth,' said his father, 'I took to the law,
   And argued each case with my wife;
And the muscular strength which it gave to my jaw
   Has lasted the rest of my life.'

'You are old,' said the youth, 'one would hardly suppose
   That your eye was as steady as ever;
Yet you balanced an eel on the end of your nose –
   What made you so awfully clever?'

'I have answered three questions, and that is enough,'
   Said his father. 'Don't give yourself airs!
Do you think I can listen all day to such stuff?
   Be off, or I'll kick you down-stairs!'

Lewis Carroll's real name was Charles Dodgson. He was a lecturer in mathematics at Oxford University, but he had a great gift for telling stories to children and often took Alice Liddell and her sisters, daughters of the Dean of Christ Church College, Oxford, on trips to the surrounding countryside, to tell them his imaginary tales. Alice encouraged him to write the stories down, and they were published as Alice's Adventures in Wonderland *and* Through the Looking Glass, *to become favourites in every generation. Dodgson also wrote children's guides to understanding mathematics, although these are less well known.*

Old father William who balances an eel on the end of his nose was inspired by Dodgson's boat trips with Alice and her sisters. They once had a picnic near to some eel traps by the Thames river at Godstow, in Oxfordshire. The children were full of tales about balancing and somersaults because they had recently seen the French acrobat Blondin perform in Oxford. Dodgson mixed their own jokes with his to conjure up this poem.

MARGARET ATWOOD
b. 1939

This Is a Photograph of Me

It was taken some time ago.
At first it seems to be
a smeared
print: blurred lines and gray flecks
blended with the paper;

then, as you scan
it, you see in the left-hand corner
a thing that is like a branch: part of a tree
(balsam or spruce) emerging
and, to the right, halfway up
what ought to be a gentle
slope, a small frame house.

In the background there is a lake,
and beyond that, some low hills.

(The photograph was taken
the day after I drowned.

I am in the lake, in the center
of the picture, just under the surface.

It is difficult to say where
precisely, or to say
how large or small I am:
the effect of water
on light is a distortion

but if you look long enough,
eventually
you will be able to see me.)

Atwood is a Canadian novelist and poet who is particularly interested in writing about women's lives. Her work is often humorous but she is also fascinated by the more serious issues surrounding the way we think about ourselves. In one of her novels, The Edible Woman, *the central character decides she wants to re-invent herself as a different kind of person, so she makes a cake of herself and eats it to mark the end of the old and the beginning of the new.*

LEWIS CARROLL
1832–1898

The White Knight's Song

I'll tell thee everything I can;
    There's little to relate.
I saw an aged, aged man,
    A-sitting on a gate.
'Who are you, aged man?' I said.
    'And how is it you live?'
And his answer trickled through my head
    Like water through a sieve.

He said 'I look for butterflies
    That sleep among the wheat;
I make them into mutton-pies,
    And sell them in the street.
I sell them unto men,' he said,
    'Who sail on stormy seas;
And that's the way I get my bread –
    A trifle, if you please.'

But I was thinking of a plan
    To dye one's whiskers green,
And always use so large a fan
    That it could not be seen.
So, having no reply to give
    To what the old man said,
I cried, 'Come, tell me how you live!'
    And thumped him on the head.

His accents mild took up the tale;
    He said, 'I go my ways,
And when I find a mountain-rill,
    I set it in a blaze;
And thence they make a stuff they call
    Rowland's Macassar Oil –
Yet twopence-halfpenny is all
    They give me for my toil.'

But I was thinking of a way
    To feed oneself on batter,
And so go on from day to day
    Getting a little fatter.
I shook him well from side to side,
    Until his face was blue;
'Come, tell me how you live,' I cried
    'And what it is you do!'

He said, 'I hunt for haddocks' eyes
    Among the heather bright,
And work them into waistcoat-buttons
    In the silent night.
And these I do not sell for gold
    Or coin of silvery shine,
But for a copper halfpenny,
    And that will purchase nine.

'I sometimes dig for buttered rolls,
    Or set limed twigs for crabs,
I sometimes search the grassy knolls
    For wheels of hansom-cabs.
And that's the way' (he gave a wink)
    'By which I get my wealth –
And very gladly will I drink
    Your Honour's noble health.'

I heard him then, for I had just
    Completed my design
To keep the Menai bridge from rust
    By boiling it in wine.
I thanked him much for telling me
    The way he got his wealth,
But chiefly for his wish that he
    Might drink my noble health.

And now, if e'er by chance I put
    My fingers into glue,
Or madly squeeze a right-hand foot
    Into a left-hand shoe,
Or if I drop upon my toe
    A very heavy weight,
I weep, for it reminds me so
Of that old man I used to know –
Whose look was mild, whose speech was slow,
Whose hair was whiter than the snow,
Whose face was very like a crow,
With eyes, like cinders, all aglow,
Who seemed distracted with his woe,
Who rocked his body to and fro,
And muttered mumblingly and low,
As if his mouth were full of dough,
Who snorted like a buffalo –
That summer evening long ago
    A-sitting on a gate.

———————

In the story Through the Looking Glass *the White Knight represents the author. He portrays himself as a chivalrous knight who looked after Alice until she was no longer a child. She then has to say goodbye to him, and to face the adult world alone.*

BENJAMIN ZEPHANIAH
b. 1958

Health Care

All yu Presidents
Think of de residents,
Queens an Kings
Start sharing,
City planners
Hav sum manners,
Prime ministers please
Think of de trees.

Those dat sail
Tek care of de whales,
De strong should seek
To strengthen de weak,
Lovers of art
Should play their part,
An all those upon it
Tek care of de planet.

ELIZABETH BARRETT BROWNING
1806–1861

Sonnet from the Portuguese

How do I love thee? Let me count the ways.
I love thee to the depth and breadth and height
My soul can reach, when feeling out of sight
For the ends of Being and ideal Grace.
I love thee to the level of everyday's
Most quiet need, by sun and candle-light.
I love thee freely, as men strive for Right;
I love thee purely, as they turn from Praise.
I love thee with the passion put to use
In my old griefs, and with my childhood's faith.
I love thee with a love I seemed to lose
With my lost saints – I love thee with the breath,
Smiles, tears, of all my life! – and if God choose,
I shall but love thee better after death.

After suffering spinal injuries in a riding accident at the age of fifteen, Elizabeth Barrett was an invalid. Her bossy father would not let her travel to Italy although it was advised that the climate could be good for her health, so she lived cooped up in a darkened room with paper on the window panes to keep out any draughts. But her vivid imagination saw her through, as did her passionate belief that poetry could change people's attitudes towards the world. She wrote poems about the plight of children working in factories and about a woman's role in Victorian England. She became the most respected English women poet of her era and was already a published poet before meeting her husband, Robert Browning. He described her personality as 'strong and peculiar'.

This is one of the poems from the Sonnets from the Portuguese *series. Her father did not approve of her relationship with Robert Browning and the couple met in secret. Robert's nickname for her was 'my little Portuguese', hence the title for the series of poems. When they eventually married her father refused to communicate with her and returned all her letters unopened*

MATTHEW ARNOLD
1822–1888

Dover Beach

The sea is calm tonight.
The tide is full, the moon lies fair
Upon the straits; on the French coast the light
Gleams and is gone; the cliffs of England stand,
Glimmering and vast, out in the tranquil bay.
Come to the window, sweet is the night-air!
Only, from the long line of spray
Where the sea meets the moon-blanched land,
Listen! you hear the grating roar
Of pebbles which the waves draw back, and fling,
At their return, up the high strand,
Begin, and cease, and then again begin,
With tremulous cadence slow, and bring
The eternal note of sadness in.

Sophocles long ago
Heard it on the Aegean, and it brought
Into his mind the turbid ebb and flow
Of human misery; we
Find also in the sound a thought,
Hearing it by this distant northern sea.

The Sea of Faith
Was once, too, at the full, and round earth's shore
Lay like the folds of a bright girdle furled.
But now I only hear
Its melancholy, long, withdrawing roar,
Retreating, to the breath
Of the night-wind, down the vast edges drear
And naked shingles of the world.

Ah, love, let us be true
To one another! for the world, which seems
To lie before us like a land of dreams,
So various, so beautiful, so new,
Hath really neither joy, nor love, nor light,
Nor certitude, nor peace, nor help for pain;
And we are here as on a darkling plain
Swept with confused alarms of struggle and flight,
Where ignorant armies clash by night.

Arnold was a schoolmaster and a school inspector before he became Professor of Poetry at Oxford University. He studied schools all over Europe and tried to encourage English schools to make children more aware of art, music, theatre and literature.

The rhythm of this poem mimics the to and fro of the waves on a sea shore. The last line was probably inspired by an account of the battle of Epipolae by the Greek historian Thucydides. In this moonlight attack soldiers could not distinguish between friend and foe.

LEWIS CARROLL
1832–1898

Jabberwocky

'Twas brillig, and the slithy toves
   Did gyre and gimble in the wabe:
All mimsy were the borogoves,
   And the mome raths outgrabe.

'Beware the Jabberwock, my son!
   The jaws that bite, the claws that catch!
Beware the Jubjub bird, and shun
   The frumious Bandersnatch!'

He took his vorpal sword in hand:
   Long time the manxome foe he sought –
So rested he by the Tumtum tree,
   And stood awhile in thought.

And, as in uffish thought he stood,
    The Jabberwock, with eyes of flame,
Came whiffling through the tulgey wood,
    And burbled as it came!

One, two! One, two! And through and through
    The vorpal blade went snicker-snack!
He left it dead, and with its head
    He went galumphing back.

'And hast thou slain the Jabberwock?
    Come to my arms, my beamish boy!
O frabjous day! Callooh! Callay!'
    He chortled in his joy.

'Twas brillig, and the slithy toves
    Did gyre and gimble in the wabe:
All mimsy were the borogoves,
    And the mome raths outgrabe.

This is a great poem about a mysterious monster. It appears in the story Through the Looking Glass. *Dodgson loved making up curious-sounding words like 'galumphing' because he rightly guessed that they made children laugh.*

JONATHAN SWIFT
1667–1745

A Description of the Morning

Now hardly here and there an hackney coach
Appearing, showed the ruddy morn's approach.
Now Betty from her master's bed had flown,
And softly stole to discompose her own;
The slipshod 'prentice from his master's door
Had pared the dirt, and sprinkled round the floor.
Now Moll had whirled her mop with dextrous airs,
Prepared to scrub the entry and the stairs.
The youth with broomy stumps began to trace
The kennel's edge, where wheels had worn the place.
The small-coal man was heard with cadence deep,
Till drowned in shriller notes of chimney sweep:
Duns at his lordship's gate began to meet;
And brickdust Moll had screamed through half the street.
The turnkey now his flock returning sees,
Duly let out a-nights to steal for fees;
The watchful bailiffs take their silent stands,
And schoolboys lag with satchels in their hands.

A satirist and clergyman, Swift, who grew up in Dublin, is best remembered for his prose. Gulliver's Travels is considered a children's book but it was written as an attack on the government of the time. In 'A Modest Proposal' the author suggests that overpopulation could be tackled by fattening up babies and eating them.

Not all Swift's writing was so fantastical, and his sense of humour was not always nasty. In this poem he uses his skill at describing realistic situations and characters. He gives a convincing impression of the buzz and frantic activities common to city life.

WILLIAM SHAKESPEARE
1564–1616

Sonnet 116

Let me not to the marriage of true minds
Admit impediments. Love is not love
Which alters when it alteration finds,
Or bends with the remover to remove.
O, no! it is an ever-fixed mark,
That looks on tempests and is never shaken;
It is the star to every wand'ring bark,
Whose worth's unknown, although his height be taken.
Love's not Time's fool, though rosy lips and cheeks
Within his bending sickle's compass come;
Love alters not with his brief hours and weeks,
But bears it out even to the edge of doom.
    If this be error, and upon me prov'd,
    I never writ, nor no man ever lov'd.

———————————

This sonnet describes an ideal kind of love between two people, which despite all the testing traumas of life, is sure to last for ever. Love which does not depend on physical attraction, but is instead a 'meeting of true minds'. It's often called Platonic love.

ALEXANDER POPE
1688–1744

Man

Selections from 'An Essay on Man'

Know then thyself, presume not God to scan,
The proper study of mankind is man.
Placed on this isthmus of a middle state,
A being darkly wise, and rudely great:
With too much knowledge for the sceptic side,
With too much weakness for the stoic's pride,
He hangs between; in doubt to act, or rest;
In doubt to deem himself a God, or beast;
In doubt his mind or body to prefer;
Born but to die, and reasoning but to err;
Alike in ignorance, his reason such,
Whether he thinks too little or too much:
Chaos of thought and passion, all confused;

Still by himself abused or disabused;
Created half to rise and half to fall;
Great lord of all things, yet a prey to all;
Sole judge of truth, in endless error hurled:
The glory, jest, and riddle of the world!
Whate'er the passion – knowledge, fame, or pelf,
Not one will change his neighbour with himself.
The learned is happy nature to explore,
The fool is happy that he knows no more;
The rich is happy in the plenty given,
The poor contents him with the care of Heaven.
See the blind beggar dance, the cripple sing,
The sot a hero, lunatic a king;
The starving chemist in his golden views,
Supremely blest, the poet in his muse.
See some strange comfort every state attend,
And pride bestowed on all, a common friend;
See some fit passion every age supply,
Hope travels through nor quits us when we die.
    Behold the child, by nature's kindly law,
Pleased with a rattle, tickled with a straw:
Some livelier play-thing gives his youth delight,
A little louder, but as empty quite:
Scarfs, garters, gold, amuse his riper stage,
And beads and prayer-books are the toys of age:
Please with this bauble still, as that before;
Till tired he sleeps, and life's poor play is o'er.

    Honour and shame from no condition rise;
Act well your part, there all the honour lies.
Fortune in men has some small difference made,
One flaunts in rags, one flutters in brocade;
The cobbler aproned, and the parson gowned,
The friar hooded, and the monarch crowned.
'What differ more [you cry] than crown and cowl!'
I'll tell you, friend! a wise man and a fool.
You'll find, if once the monarch acts the monk,
Or, cobbler-like, the parson will be drunk,
Worth makes the man, and want of it the fellow;
The rest is all but leather or prunella.

Pope achieved great fame as a writer, editor and translator. He had suffered from tuberculosis as a child and received little formal education. He was also a Roman Catholic which, in his time, meant that he was not allowed to attend university. He taught himself many subjects and formed the Scriblerus Club with other writers, including Jonathan Swift. This poem reminds us that we can never know everything. Our curiosity encourages us to seek out knowledge, but the more we know, the more aware we become of how much else there is to learn.

THOMAS GRAY
1716–1771

Elegy Written in a Country Churchyard

The curfew tolls the knell of parting day,
  The lowing herd wind slowly o'er the lea,
The ploughman homeward plods his weary way,
  And leaves the world to darkness and to me.

Now fades the glimmering landscape on the sight,
  And all the air a solemn stillness holds,
Save where the beetle wheels his droning flight,
And drowsy tinklings lull the distant folds;

Save that from yonder ivy-mantled tower
  The moping owl does to the moon complain
Of such, as wandering near her secret bower,
  Molest her ancient solitary reign.

Beneath those rugged elms, that yew tree's shade,
  Where heaves the turf in many a mouldering heap,
Each in his narrow cell forever laid,
  The rude forefathers of the hamlet sleep.

The breezy call of incense-breathing morn,
  The swallow twittering from the straw-built shed,
The cock's shrill clarion, or the echoing horn,
  No more shall rouse them from their lowly bed.

For them no more the blazing hearth shall burn,
  Or busy housewife ply her evening care;
No children run to lisp their sire's return,
  Or climb his knees the envied kiss to share.

Oft did the harvest to their sickle yield,
  Their furrow oft the stubborn glebe has broke;
How jocund did they drive their team afield!
  How bowed the woods beneath their sturdy stroke!

Let not Ambition mock their useful toil,
  Their homely joys, and destiny obscure;
Nor Grandeur hear with a disdainful smile
  The short and simple annals of the poor.

The boast of heraldry, the pomp of power,
  And all that beauty, all that wealth e'er gave,
Awaits alike the inevitable hour.
  The paths of glory lead but to the grave.

Nor you, ye proud, impute to these the fault,
  If memory o'er their tomb no trophies raise,
Where through the long-drawn aisle and fretted vault
The pealing anthem swells the note of praise.

Can storied urn or animated bust
  Back to its mansion call the fleeting breath?
Can Honour's voice provoke the silent dust,
  Or Flattery soothe the dull cold ear of Death?

Perhaps in this neglected spot is laid
  Some heart once pregnant with celestial fire;
Hands that the rod of empire might have swayed,
  Or waked to ecstasy the living lyre.

But Knowledge to their eyes her ample page
  Rich with the spoils of time did ne'er unroll;
Chill Penury repressed their noble rage,
  And froze the genial current of the soul.

Full many a gem of purest ray serene,
    The dark unfathomed caves of ocean bear:
Full many a flower is born to blush unseen,
    And waste its sweetness on the desert air.

Some village Hampden, that with dauntless breast
    The little tyrant of his fields withstood;
Some mute inglorious Milton here may rest,
    Some Cromwell guiltless of his country's blood.

The applause of listening senates to command,
    The threats of pain and ruin to despise,
To scatter plenty o'er a smiling land,
    And read their history in a nation's eyes,

Their lot forbade: nor circumscribed alone
    Their growing virtues, but their crimes confined;
Forbade to wade through slaughter to a throne,
    And shut the gates of mercy on mankind,

The struggling pangs of conscious truth to hide,
    To quench the blushes of ingenuous shame,
Or heap the shrine of Luxury and Pride
    With incense kindled at the Muse's flame.

Far from the madding crowd's ignoble strife,
    Their sober wishes never learned to stray;
Along the cool sequestered vale of life
    They kept the noiseless tenor of their way.

Yet even these bones from insult to protect
    Some frail memorial still erected nigh,
With uncouth rhymes and shapeless sculpture decked,
    Implores the passing tribute of a sigh.

Their name, their years, spelt by the unlettered Muse,
    The place of fame and elegy supply:
And many a holy text around she strews,
    That teach the rustic moralist to die.

For who to dumb Forgetfulness a prey,
　　This pleasing anxious being e'er resigned,
Left the warm precincts of the cheerful day,
　　Nor cast one longing lingering look behind?

On some fond breast the parting soul relies,
　　Some pious drops the closing eye requires;
Even from the tomb the voice of Nature cries,
　　Even in our ashes live their wonted fires.

For thee, who mindful of the unhonoured dead
　　Dost in these lines their artless tale relate;
If chance, by lonely contemplation led,
　　Some kindred spirit shall inquire thy fate,

Haply some hoary-headed swain may say,
　　'Oft have we seen him at the peep of dawn
Brushing with hasty steps the dews away
　　To meet the sun upon the upland lawn.

'There at the foot of yonder nodding beech
　　That wreathes its old fantastic roots so high,
His listless length at noontide would he stretch,
　　And pore upon the brook that babbles by.

'Hard by yon wood, now smiling as in scorn,
　　Muttering his wayward fancies he would rove,
Now drooping, woeful wan, like one forlorn,
　　Or crazed with care, or crossed in hopeless love.

'One morn I missed him on the customed hill,
　　Along the heath and near his favourite tree;
Another came; nor yet beside the rill,
　　Nor up the lawn, nor at the wood was he;

'The next with dirges due in sad array
　　Slow through the churchway path we saw him borne.
Approach and read (for thou canst read) the lay,
　　Graved on the stone beneath yon aged thorn.'

The Epitaph

Here rests his head upon the lap of Earth
  A youth to Fortune and to Fame unknown.
Fair Science frowned not on his humble birth,
  And Melancholy marked him for her own.

Large was his bounty, and his soul sincere,
  Heaven did a recompense as largely send:
He gave to Misery all he had, a tear,
  He gained from heaven ('twas all he wished) a friend.

No farther seek his merits to disclose,
  Or draw his frailties from their dread abode
(There they alike in trembling hope repose),
  The bosom of his Father and his God.

Thomas Gray was a studious poet, remembered as a student for his dislike of practical jokes. In later life he became Professor of Modern History at Cambridge University. This is his most famous poem. An elegy is usually a mournful poem written to remember the dead. In this case the poet imagines wandering among graves, and thinking about the lives of ordinary people. He wants us to remember that even though people might not achieve fame, leading an inconspicuous, worthwhile life can still be celebrated in poetry.

GEORGE GORDON, LORD BYRON
1788–1824

She Walks in Beauty

1

She walks in beauty, like the night
  Of cloudless climes and starry skies,
And all that's best of dark and bright
  Meet in her aspect and her eyes:
Thus mellowed to that tender light
  Which heaven to gaudy day denies.

2

One shade the more, one ray the less,
  Had half impaired the nameless grace
Which waves in every raven tress,
  Or softly lightens o'er her face;
Where thoughts serenely sweet express
  How pure, how dear their dwelling place.

3
And on that cheek, and o'er that brow,
   So soft, so calm, yet eloquent,
The smiles that win, the tints that glow,
   But tell of days in goodness spent,
A mind at peace with all below,
   A heart whose love is innocent!

Byron was born into an aristocratic family and took the title Sixth Baron of Rochdale. He was too outspoken and unconventional to fit comfortably into English upper class society and spent much of his life in Italy, chasing women and writing poems which usually contained a romantic hero based on himself. He considered himself lazy, but worked hard at writing as a kind of discipline.

This poem was inspired by Anne Beatrix who married Byron's cousin.

OLIVER GOLDSMITH
1730–1774

Lines from The Deserted Village

Sweet Auburn! loveliest village of the plain,
Where health and plenty cheered the labouring swain,
Where smiling spring its earliest visit paid,
And parting summer's lingering blooms delayed:
Dear lovely bowers of innocence and ease,
Seats of my youth, when every sport could please,
How often have I loitered o'er thy green,
Where humble happiness endeared each scene;
How often have I paused on every charm,
The sheltered cot, the cultivated farm,
The never-failing brook, the busy mill,
The decent church that topped the neighbouring hill,
The hawthorn bush, with seats beneath the shade,
For talking age and whispering lovers made;
How often have I blessed the coming day,
When toil remitting lent its turn to play,
And all the village train, from labour free,
Led up their sports beneath the spreading tree,
While many a pastime circled in the shade,
The young contending as the old surveyed;
And many a gambol frolicked o'er the ground,
And sleights of art and feats of strength went round;
And still as each repeated pleasure tired,
Succeeding sports the mirthful band inspired;
The dancing pair that simply sought renown,
By holding out to tire each other down;
The swain mistrustless of his smutted face,
While secret laughter tittered round the place;
The bashful virgin's sidelong looks of love,
The matron's glance that would those looks reprove:
These were thy charms, sweet village! sports like these,
With sweet succession, taught even toil to please;
These round thy bowers their cheerful influence shed,
These were thy charms – But all these charms are fled.
Sweet smiling village, loveliest of the lawn,
Thy sports are fled, and all thy charms withdrawn;

Amidst thy bowers the tyrant's hand is seen,
And desolation saddens all thy green:
One only master grasps the whole domain,
And half a tillage stints thy smiling plain;
No more thy glassy brook reflects the day,
But choked with sedges, works its weedy way;
Along thy glades, a solitary guest,
The hollow-sounding bittern guards its nest;
Amidst thy desert walks the lapwing flies,
And tires their echoes with unvaried cries.
Sunk are thy bowers, in shapeless ruin all,
And the long grass o'ertops the mouldering wall,
And, trembling, shrinking from the spoiler's hand,
Far, far away thy children leave the land.

This poem was written at a time when many people in England were moving out of villages and into towns. Industrialization was changing traditional rural life and people were moving to find jobs. The poet is keen to remember what village life was like when he was a child but he also wants to express his opinion about the obsession with material goods and the pursuit of luxury. The village he refers to in this poem as 'Sweet Auburn' is thought to be based on the Oxfordshire village of Nuneham Courtney. The local landowner had forced the population to move because they upset the appearance of his beautifully landscaped park.

EDWARD TAYLOR
1644–1729

Upon a Spider Catching a Fly

Thou sorrow, venom elf:
　　Is this thy play,
To spin a web out of thyself
　　To catch a fly?
　　　For why?

I saw a pettish wasp
　　Fall foul therein,
Whom yet thy whorl-pins did not clasp
　　Lest he should fling
　　　His sting.

But as afraid, remote
　　Didst stand hereat
And with thy little fingers stroke
　　And gently tap
　　　His back.

Thus gently him didst treat
　　Lest he should pet,
And in a froppish, waspish heat
　　Should greatly fret
　　　Thy net.

Whereas the silly fly,
　　Caught by its leg
Thou by the throat tookst hastily
　　And hind the head
　　　Bite dead.

This goes to pot, that not
　　Nature doth call.
Strive not above what strength hath got
　　Lest in the brawl
　　　Thou fall.

This fray seems thus to us.
    Hell's spider gets
His entrails spun to whip-cords thus,
    And wove to nets
        And sets.

To tangle Adam's race
    In's strategems
To their destructions, spoiled, made base
    By venom things,
        Damned sins.

But mighty, gracious Lord
    Communicate
Thy grace to break the cord, afford
    Us glory's gate
        And state.

We'll nightingale sing like
    When perched on high
In glory's cage, thy glory, bright,
    And thankfully,
        For joy.

ROBERT BURNS
1759–1796

John Anderson, My Jo

John Anderson my jo, John,
    When we were first acquent,
Your locks were like the raven,
    Your bonie brow was brent;
But now your brow is beld, John,
    Your locks are like the snow;
But blessings on your frosty pow,
    John Anderson, my jo.

John Anderson, my jo, John,
    We clamb the hill thegither;
And mony a canty day, John,
    We've had wi' ane anither:
Now we maun totter down, John,
    And hand in hand we'll go,
And sleep thegither at the foot,
    John Anderson, my jo.

———————

Robert Burns married Jean Armour in 1788. They had a family but he was not a faithful husband, and had many affairs and several children in other relationships. However, this poem is a tribute to fidelity and the kind of love that you feel for someone with whom you have lived for a long time. The couple remember their carefree youth, but they are also happy to have faced the struggles of life together.

WILLIAM BLAKE
1757–1827

(Lines from *Jerusalem*)

England! Awake! Awake! Awake!

England! awake! awake! awake!
 Jerusalem thy Sister calls!
Why wilt thou sleep the sleep of death?
 And close her from thy ancient walls.

Thy hills & valleys felt her feet,
 Gently upon their bosoms move:
Thy gates beheld sweet Zions ways;
 Then was a time of joy and love.

And now the time returns again:
 Our souls exult & Londons towers,
Receive the Lamb of God to dwell
 In Englands green & pleasant bowers.

———————

Blake was interested in the politics of his time and supported the American and French Revolutions. In his long poem Jerusalem, *of which this text is a fragment, he longs to build a place like Heaven on English soil. He asks whether religion and politics are really the same thing and whether the real aim is to build a brotherhood of man that brings unity and mutual forgiveness. Only one coloured copy of the book of* Jerusalem *existed, and at the time of Blake's death it was still unsold. It was only in the twentieth century that Blake began to be prized as a serious, visionary artist and writer.*

WILLIAM SHAKESPEARE
1564–1616

Lines from Hamlet

To be, or not to be – that is the question;
Whether 'tis nobler in the mind to suffer
The slings and arrows of outrageous fortune,
Or to take arms against a sea of troubles,
And by opposing end them? To die, to sleep –
No more; and by a sleep to say we end
The heart-ache and the thousand natural shocks
That flesh is heir to. 'Tis a consummation
Devoutly to be wish'd. To die, to sleep;
To sleep, perchance to dream. Ay, there's the rub;
For in that sleep of death what dreams may come,
When we have shuffled off this mortal coil,
Must give us pause. There's the respect
That makes calamity of so long life;
For who would bear the whips and scorns of time,
Th' oppressor's wrong, the proud man's contumely,
The pangs of despis'd love, the law's delay,
The insolence of office, and the spurns
That patient merit of th' unworthy takes,
When he himself might his quietus make
With a bare bodkin? Who would these fardels bear,
To grunt and sweat under a weary life,
But that the dread of something after death –
The undiscover'd country, from whose bourn
No traveller returns – puzzles the will,
And makes me rather bear those ills we have
Than fly to others that we know not of?
Thus conscience does make cowards of us all;
And thus the native hue of resolution
Is sicklied o'er with the pale cast of thought,
And enterprises of great pitch and moment,
With this regard, their currents turn awry
And lose the name of action. – Soft you now!
The fair Ophelia. – Nymph, in thy orisons
Be all my sins rememb'red.

ALFRED, LORD TENNYSON
1809–1892

Lines from The Lady of Shalott

PART IV

In the stormy east-wind straining,
The pale yellow woods were waning,
The broad stream in his banks complaining,
Heavily the low sky raining
    Over tower'd Camelot;
Down she came and found a boat
Beneath a willow left afloat,
And round about the prow she wrote
    The Lady of Shalott.

And down the river's dim expanse,
Like some bold seer in a trance,
Seeing all his own mischance –
With a glassy countenance
    Did she look to Camelot.
And at the closing of the day
She loosed the chain, and down she lay;
The broad stream bore her far away,
    The Lady of Shalott.

Lying, robed in snowy white
That loosely flew to left and right –
The leaves upon her falling light –
Thro' the noises of the night
    She floated down to Camelot:
And as the boat-head wound along
The willowy hills and fields among,
They heard her singing her last song,
    The Lady of Shalott.

Heard a carol, mournful, holy,
Chanted loudly, chanted lowly,
Till her blood was frozen slowly,
And her eyes were darken'd wholly,
    Turn'd to tower'd Camelot.
For ere she reach'd upon the tide
The first house by the water-side,
Singing in her song she died,
    The Lady of Shalott.

Under tower and balcony,
By garden-wall and gallery,
A gleaming shape she floated by,
Dead-pale between the houses high,
    Silent into Camelot.
Out upon the wharfs they came,
Knight and burgher, lord and dame,
And round the prow they read her name,
    The Lady of Shalott.

Who is this? and what is here?
And in the lighted palace near
Died the sound of royal cheer;
And they cross'd themselves for fear,
    All the knights at Camelot:
But Lancelot mused a little space;
He said, 'She has a lovely face;
God in his mercy lend her grace,
    The Lady of Shalott.'

Based on the Arthurian legend and the Italian story 'Donna di Scalotta', this poem is a parable. A young weaver is imprisoned in a tower and forbidden to look out of the window. Lancelot visits her and she gives up her work, which is then torn from her loom. With this story, Tennyson suggests that a solitary life might prevent people from growing up, and coping with the outside world. Freedom and love may bring joy, but we can never escape the fact that such a choice might destroy other things which matter.

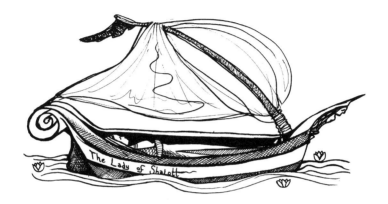

WILLIAM BUTLER YEATS
1865–1939

The Second Coming

Turning and turning in the widening gyre
The falcon cannot hear the falconer;
Things fall apart; the centre cannot hold;
Mere anarchy is loosed upon the world,
The blood-dimmed tide is loosed, and everywhere
The ceremony of innocence is drowned;
The best lack all conviction, while the worst
Are full of passionate intensity.

Surely some revelation is at hand;
Surely the Second Coming is at hand:
The Second Coming! Hardly are those words out
When a vast image out of *Spiritus Mundi*
Troubles my sight: somewhere in sands of the desert
A shape with lion body and the head of a man,
A gaze blank and pitiless as the sun,
Is moving its slow thighs, while all about it
Reel shadows of the indignant desert birds.
The darkness drops again; but now I know
That twenty centuries of stony sleep
Were vexed to nightmare by a rocking cradle,
And what rough beast, its hour come round at last,
Slouches towards Bethlehem to be born?

Yeats was born in Dublin, of a Protestant family, and his poetry always reflected a strong interest in Irish culture. In 1892 he founded the Irish National Literature Society which set out to promote Irish literature as distinct from English literature. In 1924 he was awarded the Nobel Prize.

This poem was written in 1922 and is sometimes seen as Yeats's prophecy of the rise of Fascism and Nazism between the two World Wars.

EARLE BIRNEY
b. 1904

The Bear on the Delhi Road

Unreal   tall as a myth
by the road the Himalayan bear
is beating the brilliant air
with his crooked arms
About him two men   bare
spindly as locusts   leap
One pulls on a ring
in the great soft nose   His mate
flicks   flicks with a stick
up at the rolling eyes

They have not led him here
down from the fabulous hills
to this bald alien plain
and the clamorous world   to kill
but simply to teach him to dance

They are peaceful both   these spare
men of Kashmir   and the bear
alive is their living   too
If   far on the Delhi way
around him galvanic they dance
it is merely to wear   wear
from his shaggy body the tranced
wish forever to stay
only an ambling bear
four-footed in berries

It is no more joyous for them
in this hot dust to prance
out of reach of the praying claws
sharpened to paw for ants
in the shadows of deodars
It is not easy to free
myth from reality
or rear this fellow up
to lurch   lurch with them
in the tranced dancing of men

———————————

Birney is one of Canada's most famous poets. He was an only child and spent the first seven years of his life in a remote region of Alberta with no play mates. Not surprisingly when he began to write, his poems were about the natural world, loneliness and about the difficult decisions which we all, in time, must confront.

RICHARD LOVELACE
1618–1658

To Althea, from Prison

When Love with unconfinéd wings
Hovers within my gates,
And my divine Althea brings
To whisper at the grates;
When I lie tangled in her hair
And fettered to her eye,
The gods that wanton in the air
Know no such liberty.

When flowing cups run swiftly round,
With no allaying Thames,
Our careless heads with roses bound,
Our hearts with loyal flames;
When thirsty grief in wine we steep,
When healths and draughts go free,
Fishes, that tipple in the deep,
Know no such liberty.

When, like committed linnets, I
With shriller throat shall sing
The sweetness, mercy, majesty,
And glories of my King;
When I shall voice aloud how good
He is, how great should be,
Enlargéd winds, that curl the flood,
Know no such liberty.

Stone walls do not a prison make,
Nor iron bars a cage;
Minds innocent and quiet take
That for an hermitage.
If I have freedom in my love,
And in my soul am free,
Angels alone, that soar above,
Enjoy such liberty.

Lovelace was a wealthy and handsome supporter of Charles I and was imprisoned when Cromwell and the Puritans came to power. Prison brought loneliness and misery as he was separated from the people he loved. So he spent his time writing poetry to express his frustration. In this poem Lovelace argues that prison cannot prevent the freedom to love, even if it does restrict freedom of movement. He also says that in life beyond the prison walls, with total freedom, we still take love for granted and forget what it is to care about someone.

CHRISTOPHER MARLOWE
1564–1593

The Passionate Shepherd to His Love

Come live with me and be my Love,
And we will all the pleasures prove
That valleys, groves, hills, and fields,
Woods, or steepy mountains yields.

And we will sit upon the rocks
Seeing the shepherds feed their flocks,
By shallow rivers, to whose falls
Melodious birds sing madrigals.

And I will make thee beds of roses
And a thousand fragrant posies,
A cap of flowers, and a kirtle
Embroidered all with leaves of myrtle;

A gown made of the finest wool,
Which from our pretty lambs we pull;
Fair linèd slippers for the cold,
With buckles of the purest gold;

A belt of straw and ivy buds
With coral clasps and amber studs;
And if these pleasures may thee move,
Come live with me and be my Love.

The shepherd swains shall dance and sing
For thy delight each May morning:
If these delights thy mind may move,
Then live with me and be my Love.

Christopher Marlowe was a friend of Walter Ralegh's and another member of 'The School of the Night'. He wrote poetry and plays and worked as a spy for the Protestant Queen Elizabeth I, trying to protect her from plots by Catholic assassins. Marlowe died in a mysterious fight in south London which almost certainly had something to do with his spying.

Here the poet assumes the role of a shepherd trying to persuade a nymph that his love for her will last for ever and that they will both be happy if they live in the peaceful countryside. Sir Walter Ralegh wrote another poem entitled 'The Nymph's Reply to the Shepherd'. In that poem the nymph suggests that she cannot believe in everlasting love. She suspects that when her beauty fades the shepherd will want to find another.

JOHN MILTON
1608–1674

Sonnet xix

ON HIS BLINDNESS

When I consider how my light is spent
Ere half my days in this dark world and wide,
And that one talent which is death to hide
Lodged with me useless, though my soul more bent
To serve therewith my Maker, and present
My true account, lest He returning chide;
'Doth God exact day-labour, light denied?'
I fondly ask. But Patience, to prevent
That murmur, soon replies, 'God doth not need
Either man's work or his own gifts. Who best
Bear his mild yoke, they serve him best. His state
Is kingly: thousands at his bidding speed,
And post o'er land and ocean without rest;
They also serve who only stand and wait.'

e.e. cummings
1894–1962

r-p-o-p-h-e-s-s-a-g-r

r-p-o-p-h-e-s-s-a-g-r
                who
a)s w(e loo)k
upnowgath
            PPEGORHRASS
                        eringint (o-
aThe):l
      eA
         !p:
S   a
              (r
rIvInG   .gRrEaPsPhOs)
                                    to
rea (be) rran (com) gi (e) ngly
,grasshopper;

ALFRED, LORD TENNYSON
1809–1892

The Lotos-Eaters

'Courage!' he said, and pointed toward the land,
'This mounting wave will roll us shoreward soon.'
In the afternoon they came unto a land
In which it seemed always afternoon.
All round the coast the languid air did swoon,
Breathing like one that hath a weary dream.
Full-faced above the valley stood the moon;
And like a downward smoke, the slender stream
Along the cliff to fall and pause and fall did seem.

A land of streams! some, like a downward smoke
Slow-dropping veils of thinnest lawn, did go;
And some thro' wavering lights and shadows broke,
Rolling a slumbrous sheet of foam below.
They saw the gleaming river seaward flow
From the inner land: far off, three mountain-tops,
Three silent pinnacles of aged snow,
Stood sunset-flush'd: and, dew'd with showery drops,
Up-clomb the shadowy pine above the woven copse.

The charmed sunset linger'd low adown
In the red West: thro' mountain clefts the dale
Was seen far inland and the yellow down
Border'd with palm, and many a winding vale
And meadow, set with slender galingale;
A land where all things always seem'd the same!
And round about the keel with faces pale,
Dark faces pale against that rosy flame,
The mild-eyed melancholy Lotos-eaters came.

Branches they bore of that enchanted stem,
Laden with flower and fruit, whereof they gave
To each, but whoso did receive of them,
And taste, to him the gushing of the wave
Far far away did seem to mourn and rave
On alien shores; and if his fellow spake,
His voice was thin, as voices from the grave;
And deep-asleep he seem'd, yet all awake,
And music in his ears his beating heart did make.

They sat them down upon the yellow sand,
Between the sun and moon upon the shore;
And sweet it was to dream of Fatherland,
Of child, and wife, and slave; but evermore
Most weary seem'd the sea, weary the oar,
Weary the wandering fields of barren foam.
Then some one said, 'We will return no more';
And all at once they sang, 'Our island home
Is far beyond the wave; we will no longer roam.'

This poem is based on an incident in the Odyssey, *an ancient Greek story
by Homer. Certain characters in the story eat magic flowers which make
them forget where home is.*

FEDERICO GARCÍA LORCA
1899–1936

The Six Strings

The guitar
makes dreams cry.
The crying of lost
souls
escapes from its round
mouth.
And like the tarantula
it weaves a huge star
to catch sighs
that float on its black
wooden tank.

(trans. Donald Hall)

WILFRED WILSON GIBSON
1878–1962

All Being Well

All being well, I'll come to you,
Sweetheart, before the year is through;
And we shall find so much to do,
So much to tell.

I read your letter through and through,
And dreamt of all we'd say and do,
Till in my heart the thought of you
Rang like a bell.

Now the bell tolls, my love, for you;
For long before the year is through
You've gone where there is naught to do
And naught to tell.

Yet mayn't I find when life is through
The best is still to say and do,
When I at last may come to you,
All being well?

JOHN MILTON
1608–1674

Lines from *Paradise Lost*

BOOK I: THE INVOCATION

Of man's first disobedience, and the fruit
Of that forbidden tree whose mortal taste
Brought death into the world, and all our woe,
With loss of Eden, till one greater Man

Restore us, and regain the blissful seat,
Sing, Heavenly Muse, that, on the secret top
Of Oreb, or Sinai, didst inspire
That shepherd who first taught the chosen seed

In the beginning how the Heavens and Earth
Rose out of Chaos: or, if Sion hill
Delight thee more, and Siloa's brook that flowed
Fast by the oracle of God, I thence
Invoke thy aid to my adventurous song,
That with no middle flight intends to soar
Above th' Aonian mount, while it pursues
Things unattempted yet in prose or rhyme.
And chiefly thou, O Spirit, that dost prefer
Before all temples th' upright heart and pure,
Instruct me, for thou know'st; thou from the first
Wast present, and, with mighty wings outspread,
Dovelike sat'st brooding on the vast abyss,
And mad'st it pregnant: what in me is dark
Illumine; what is low, raise and support;
That, to the height of this great argument,
I may assert Eternal Providence,
And justify the ways of God to men.

THEODORE ROETHKE
1908–1963

The Meadow Mouse

I

In a shoe box stuffed in an old nylon stocking
Sleeps the baby mouse I found in the meadow,
Where he trembled and shook beneath a stick
Till I caught him up by the tail and brought him in,
Cradled in my hand,
A little quaker, the whole body of him trembling,
His absurd whiskers sticking out like a cartoon-mouse,
His feet like small leaves,
Little lizard-feet,
Whitish and spread wide when he tried to struggle away,
Wriggling like a miniscule puppy.

Now he's eaten his three kinds of cheese and drunk from his
    bottle-cap watering-trough –
So much he just lies in one corner,
His tail curled under him, his belly big
As his head, his bat-like ears
Twitching, tilting toward the least sound.

Do I imagine he no longer trembles
When I come close to him?
He seems no longer to tremble.

II

But this morning the shoe-box house on the back porch is empty.
Where has he gone, my meadow mouse,
My thumb of a child that nuzzled in my palm? –
To run under the hawk's wing,
Under the eye of the great owl watching from the elm-tree,
To live by courtesy of the shrike, the snake, the tom-cat.

I think of the nestling fallen into the deep grass,
The turtle gasping in the dusty rubble of the highway,
The paralytic stunned in the tub, and the water rising, –
All things innocent, hapless, forsaken.

GEORGE HERBERT
1593–1633

Love (III)

Love bade me welcome: yet my soul drew back,
    Guilty of dust and sin.
But quick-eyed Love, observing me grow slack
    From my first entrance in,
Drew nearer to me, sweetly questioning
    If I lacked anything.

'A guest,' I answered, 'worthy to be here':
    Love said, 'You shall be he.'
'I, the unkind, ungrateful? Ah, my dear,
    I cannot look on thee.'
Love took my hand, and smiling did reply,
    'Who made the eyes but I?'

'Truth, Lord; but I have marred them; let my shame
    Go where it doth deserve.'
'And know you not,' says Love, 'who bore the blame?'
    'My dear, then I will serve.'
'You must sit down,' says Love, 'and taste my meat.'
    So I did sit and eat.

Herbert was a Metaphysical poet. He was influenced by John Donne who was a friend of his mother's. Herbert's poems appear to be simpler than Donne's and they usually have a more musical rythmn.

This poem takes the form of a conversation between Herbert and Jesus. Herbert's poems were not published in his lifetime, and on his deathbed he gave his collected writings to a friend with instructions to publish. This poem was the last in his published collection of poetry, entitled The Temple. *He described the volume as 'a picture of spiritual conflicts between God and my soul'.*

SEAMUS HEANEY
b. 1939

The Peninsula

When you have nothing more to say, just drive
For a day all round the peninsula.
The sky is tall as over a runway,
The land without marks, so you will not arrive

But pass through, though always skirting landfall.
At dusk, horizons drink down sea and hill,
The ploughed field swallows the whitewashed gable
And you're in the dark again. Now recall

The glazed foreshore and silhouetted log,
That rock where breakers shredded into rags,
The leggy birds stilted on their own legs,
Islands riding themselves out into the fog,

And drive back home, still with nothing to say
Except that now you will uncode all landscapes
By this: things founded clean on their own shapes,
Water and ground in their extremity.

Heaney was born in County Derry in Northern Ireland and was influenced by the work of William Wordsworth, Thomas Hardy, Robert Frost and Ted Hughes. Many of his poems deal with the earth and rural landscapes but he writes with great passion too about the age old conflict in Ireland between Protestant and Catholic. Heaney lost several friends in Irish terrorist killings and has dedicated poems to them. He was awarded the Nobel Prize for Literature in 1995.

WILLIAM BLAKE
1757–1827

The Tyger

Tyger! Tyger! burning bright
In the forests of the night,
What immortal hand or eye
Could frame thy fearful symmetry?

In what distant deeps or skies
Burnt the fire of thine eyes?
On what wings dare he aspire?
What the hand, dare seize the fire?

And what shoulder, & what art,
Could twist the sinews of thy heart?
And when thy heart began to beat,
What dread hand? & what dread feet?

What the hammer? what the chain?
In what furnace was thy brain?
What the anvil? what dread gasp
Dare its deadly terrors clasp?

When the stars threw down their spears,
And water'd heaven with their tears,
Did he smile his work to see?
Did he who made the Lamb make thee?

Tyger! Tyger! burning bright
In the forests of the night,
What immortal hand or eye
Dare frame thy fearful symmetry?

The Songs of Experience *contrast with* The Songs of Innocence *and there is a matching opposite poem in each collection. The poem 'The Lamb' matches 'The Tyger'. The songs were inspired by the desire to make a comparison between an adult's experience of real life and the innocence of a child. Blake reminds us that the same God made ferocious creatures like the tiger, as well as gentle lambs.*

JOHN DRYDEN
1631–1700

Song from THE INDIAN EMPEROR

Ah, fading joy, how quickly art thou past!
　Yet we thy ruin haste.
As if the cares of human life were few,
　We seek out new:
And follow fate, which would too fast pursue.

See how on every bough the birds express
　In their sweet notes their happiness.
　They all enjoy and nothing spare;
But on their mother nature lay their care:
Why then should man, the lord of all below,
　Such troubles choose to know
As none of all his subjects undergo?

Hark, hark the waters fall, fall, fall,
　And with a murmuring sound
　Dash, dash upon the ground,
　　To gentle slumber's call.

———————

Dryden, the poet and playwright, favoured a clear and simple style of writing. Theatrical plays were banned under Cromwell but revived at the Restoration when Charles II came to the throne. The play from which this song comes is about the conquest of Mexico by the Spaniards.

GWENDOLYN BROOKS
b. 1917

The Bean Eaters

They eat beans mostly, this old yellow pair.
Dinner is a casual affair.
Plain chipware on a plain and creaking wood,
Tin flatware.

Two who are Mostly Good.
Two who have lived their day,
But keep on putting on their clothes
And putting things away.

And remembering . . .
Remembering, with twinklings and twinges,
As they lean over the beans in their rented back room that is full of
    beads and receipts and dolls and clothes, tobacco crumbs, vases and
    fringes.

———————

The African-American poet, Gwendolyn Brooks, was born in Kansas, in the United States. Since 1968 she has worked hard to fight racial discrimination and to improve life for young black Americans.

MANILA KOORDADA
mid–20th century

You Can't Escape Your Life Record

In this dream I walked
and then sat down in an area.
Suddenly, they ambushed me

with jabiri, spears.
They came from everywhere
until I was surrounded
by all those people with spears.
I couldn't escape.

There's a history kept on you.
All your life's actions can look at you like spears.
You can't escape your life record.
The spear-holders are all spirit men,
they make you face your life record after you die.

HENRY WADSWORTH LONGFELLOW
1807–1882

The Day is Done

The day is done, and the darkness
   Falls from the wings of Night,
As a feather is wafted downward
   From an eagle in his flight.

I see the lights of the village
   Gleam through the rain and the mist,
And a feeling of sadness comes o'er me
   That my soul cannot resist:

A feeling of sadness and longing,
   That is not akin to pain,
And resembles sorrow only
   As the mist resembles the rain.

Come, read to me some poem,
   Some simple and heartfelt lay,
That shall soothe this restless feeling,
   And banish the thoughts of day.

Not from the grand old masters,
   Not from the bards sublime,
Whose distant footsteps echo
   Through the corridors of Time.

For, like strains of martial music,
   Their mighty thoughts suggest
Life's endless toil and endeavour;
   And to-night I long for rest.

Read from some humbler poet,
   Whose songs gushed from his heart,
As showers from the clouds of summer,
   Or tears from the eyelids start:

Who, through long days of labour,
And nights devoid of ease,
Still heard in his soul the music
Of wonderful melodies.

Such songs have power to quiet
The restless pulse of care,
And come like the benediction
That follows after prayer.

Then read from the treasured volume
The poem of thy choice,
And lend to the rhyme of the poet
The beauty of thy voice.

And the night shall be filled with music,
And the cares, that infest the day,
Shall fold their tents, like the Arabs,
And as silently steal away.

Longfellow was an American writer who was involved in the anti-slavery campaigns. He had grown up in remote countryside in the state of Maine and its forests and coastline fired his imagination and encouraged him to write.

ROBERT DESNOS
1900–1945

No, Love is not Dead

No, love is not dead in this heart and these eyes and this mouth that proclaimed the beginning of its own requiem.

Listen, I've had enough of the picturesque, of colors and charm.

I love love, its tenderness and its cruelty.

The one I love has only a single name, a single form.

Everything goes. Mouths cling to this mouth.

The one I love has only one name, one form.

And some day if you remember it

O you, form and name of my love,

One day on the sea between America and Europe,

When the last ray of sun flashes on the undulating surface of the waves, or else one stormy night beneath a tree in the country, or in a speeding car,

One spring morning Boulevard Malesherbes,

One rainy day,

At dawn before putting yourself to bed,

Tell yourself, I summon your familiar ghost, that I was the only one to love you more and what a pity it is you didn't know it.

Tell yourself you shouldn't be sorry for anything: before me Ronsard and Baudelaire sang the sorrows of old women and dead women who despised the purest love.

You, when you die,

You will still be beautiful and desirable.

I'll already be dead, completely enclosed in your immortal body, in your astonishing image present forever among the perpetual wonders of life and eternity, but if I outlive you

Your voice and how it sounds, your gaze and how it shines,

The smell of you and of your hair and many other things will still go on living in me,

In me, and I'm no Ronsard or Baudelaire,

Just me Robert Desnos who, for having known and loved you,

Is as good as they are.

Just me Robert Desnos who, for loving you

Doesn't want to be remembered for anything else on this despicable earth.

(trans. Bill Zavatsky)

JOHN DONNE
1573–1631

Song

Go and catch a falling star,
    Get with child a mandrake root,
Tell me where all past years are,
    Or who cleft the Devil's foot,
Teach me to hear mermaids singing,
Or to keep off envy's stinging,
                And find
                What wind
Serves to advance an honest mind.

If thou beest born to strange sights,
    Things invisible to see,
Ride ten thousand days and nights,
    Till age snow white hairs on thee.
Thou, when thou return'st, wilt tell me
All strange wonders that befell thee,
                And swear
                Nowhere
Lives a woman true, and fair.

If thou find'st one, let me know,
    Such a pilgrimage were sweet;
Yet do not, I would not go,
    Though at next door we might meet;
Though she were true when you met her,
And last till you write your letter,
                Yet she
                Will be
False, ere I come, to two, or three.

This is a poem about the inconsistencies of women. The poet implies, in a humorous way, that no woman will forever stay in love with a man. She will always be changing her mind. Donne was devoted to his own wife, whom he had married secretly when she was just sixteen. He had been working as secretary to the Keeper of the Great Seal and fell in love with the niece of his employer's wife. The relationship upset the family and Donne lost his job.

The Fish

I caught a tremendous fish
and held him beside the boat
half out of water, with my hook
fast in a corner of his mouth.
He didn't fight.
He hadn't fought at all.
He hung a grunting weight,
battered and venerable
and homely. Here and there
his brown skin hung in strips
like ancient wallpaper,
and its pattern of darker brown
was like wallpaper:
shapes like full-blown roses
stained and lost through age.
He was speckled with barnacles,
fine rosettes of lime,
and infested
with tiny white sea-lice,
and underneath two or three
rags of green weed hung down.
While his gills were breathing in
the terrible oxygen
– the frightening gills,
fresh and crisp with blood,
that can cut so badly –
I thought of the coarse white flesh
packed in like feathers,
the big bones and the little bones,
the dramatic reds and blacks
of his shiny entrails,
and the pink swim-bladder
like a big peony.
I looked into his eyes
which were far larger than mine
but shallower, and yellowed,

166

the irises backed and packed
with tarnished tinfoil
seen through the lenses
of old scratched isinglass.
They shifted a little, but not
to return my stare.
— It was more like the tipping
of an object toward the light.
I admired his sullen face,
the mechanism of his jaw,
and then I saw
that from his lower lip
— if you could call it a lip —
grim, wet, and weaponlike,
hung five old pieces of fish-line,
or four and a wire leader
with the swivel still attached,
with all their five big hooks
grown firmly in his mouth.
A green line, frayed at the end
where he broke it, two heavier lines,
and a fine black thread
still crimped from the strain and snap
when it broke and he got away.
Like medals with their ribbons
frayed and wavering,
a five-haired beard of wisdom
trailing from his aching jaw.
I stared and stared
and victory filled up
the little rented boat,
from the pool of bilge
where oil had spread a rainbow
around the rusted engine
to the bailer rusted orange,
the sun-cracked thwarts,
the oarlocks on their strings,
the gunnels — until everything
was rainbow, rainbow, rainbow!
And I let the fish go.

WILLIAM BUTLER YEATS
1865–1939

When You Are Old

When you are old and grey and full of sleep,
And nodding by the fire, take down this book,
And slowly read, and dream of the soft look
Your eyes had once, and of their shadows deep;

How many loved your moments of glad grace,
And loved your beauty with love false or true,
But one man loved the pilgrim soul in you,
And loved the sorrows of your changing face;

And bending down beside the glowing bars,
Murmur, a little sadly, how Love fled
And paced upon the mountains overhead
And hid his face amid a crowd of stars.

WILLIAM CARLOS WILLIAMS
1883–1963

This Is Just to Say

I have eaten
the plums
that were in
the icebox

and which
you were probably
saving
for breakfast

Forgive me
they were delicious
so sweet
and so cold

―――――――――

Williams was a children's doctor and a poet. One story describes his suddenly having an idea for a poem as he is driving to a house to visit a sick child. He pulls over to the side of the road and scribbles lines on a blank prescription, before continuing his journey. Many of the poems he wrote in the 1930s and 1940s have a despairing tone because he was appalled by the racist policies of the Nazi and Fascist regimes.

OSCAR WILDE
1854–1900

Lines from The Ballad of Reading Gaol

In Reading gaol by Reading town
　　There is a pit of shame,
And in it lies a wretched man
　　Eaten by teeth of flame,
In a burning winding-sheet he lies,
　　And his grave has got no name.

And there, till Christ call forth the dead,
　　In silence let him lie:
No need to waste the foolish tear,
　　Or heave the windy sigh:
The man had killed the thing he loved,
　　And so he had to die.

And all men kill the thing they love,
　　By all let this be heard,
Some do it with a bitter look,
　　Some with a flattering word,
The coward does it with a kiss,
　　The brave man with a sword!

Born in Dublin, Oscar Wilde was famous for his witty plays such as The Importance of Being Earnest. *He became a larger than life character in London society, wearing flamboyant velvet and silk outfits and making fun of people who, in his view, took themselves too seriously or who were afraid to be individuals. His lifestyle changed dramatically when he was prosecuted in court for his sexual relationship with a young aristocrat, Lord Alfred Douglas. Homosexual relationships between men were against the law in Victorian England, and he was sentenced to two years hard labour in Reading gaol.*

Wilde wrote this poem while he was in prison. He was kept in solitary confinement for two years; utter torment for a man who had once expressed his wish to do nothing in life, but to have discussions. This ballad is his only piece of fictional writing which draws directly on his experience of real life.

THOMAS HARDY
1840–1928

The Darkling Thrush

I leant upon a coppice gate
    When Frost was spectre-gray,
And Winter's dregs made desolate
    The weakening eye of day.
The tangled bine-stems scored the sky
    Like strings of broken lyres,
And all mankind that haunted nigh
    Had sought their household fires.

The land's sharp features seemed to be
    The Century's corpse outleant,
His crypt the cloudy canopy,
    The wind his death-lament.
The ancient pulse of germ and birth
    Was shrunken hard and dry,
And every spirit upon earth
    Seemed fervourless as I.

At once a voice arose among
    The bleak twigs overhead
In a full-hearted evensong
    Of joy illimited;
An aged thrush, frail, gaunt, and small,
    In blast-beruffled plume,
Had chosen thus to fling his soul
    Upon the growing gloom.

So little cause for carolings
    Of such ecstatic sound
Was written on terrestrial things
    Afar or nigh around,
That I could think there trembled through
    His happy goodnight air
Some blessed Hope, whereof he knew
    And I was unaware.

172

BEN JONSON
1572–1637

'It is not growing like a tree'

It is not growing like a tree
In bulk, doth make Man better be;
Or standing long an oak, three hundred year,
To fall a log at last, dry, bald, and sere:
A lily of a day
Is fairer far in May,
Although it fall and die that night;
It was the plant and flower of Light.
In small proportions we just beauties see;
And in short measures life may perfect be.

EDWARD THOMAS
1878–1917

Adlestrop

Yes. I remember Adlestrop –
The name, because one afternoon
Of heat the express-train drew up there
Unwontedly. It was late June.

The steam hissed. Someone cleared his throat.
No one left and no one came
On the bare platform. What I saw
Was Adlestrop – only the name.

And willows, willow-herb, and grass,
And meadowsweet, and haycocks dry,
No whit less still and lonely fair
Than the high cloudlets in the sky.

And for that minute a blackbird sang
Close by, and round him, mistier,
Farther and farther, all the birds
Of Oxfordshire and Gloucestershire.

━━━━━━━━━━━━

Edward Thomas began writing poetry in 1914, the year the First World War began. He was encouraged by the American poet Robert Frost. His poetry expressed the disappointment that many men of his generation felt – a sense of being out of place in society. He hoped that once the war was over, there would be a new optimism and a true sense of community. Sadly, he was killed in battle in 1917.

LESLIE MARMON SILKO
b. 1948

How to Write a Poem about the Sky

FOR THE STUDENTS OF THE BETHEL MIDDLE SCHOOL,
BETHEL, ALASKA – FEB. 1975

You can see the sky now
colder than the frozen river
so dense and white
little birds
walk across it.

You see the sky now
but the earth
is lost in it
and there are no horizons.
It is all
a single breath.

You see sky
but the earth is called
by the same name
              the moment
              the wind shifts
sun splits it open
and bluish membranes
push through slits of skin.

You see the sky

JOHN KEATS
1795–1821

Ode to a Nightingale

1

My heart aches, and a drowsy numbness pains
  My sense, as though of hemlock I had drunk,
Or emptied some dull opiate to the drains
  One minute past, and Lethe-wards had sunk:
'Tis not through envy of thy happy lot,
  But being too happy in thine happiness –
    That thou, light-wingéd Dryad of the trees,
      In some melodious plot
  Of beechen green, and shadows numberless,
    Singest of summer in full-throated ease.

2

O, for a draught of vintage! that hath been
  Cooled a long age in the deep-delvéd earth,
Tasting of Flora and the country green,
  Dance, and Provençal song, and sunburnt mirth!
O for a beaker full of the warm South,
  Full of the true, the blushful Hippocrene,
    With beaded bubbles winking at the brim,
      And purple-stainéd mouth;
  That I might drink, and leave the world unseen,
    And with thee fade away into the forest dim:

3

Fade far away, dissolve, and quite forget
  What thou among the leaves hast never known,
The weariness, the fever, and the fret
  Here, where men sit and hear each other groan;
Where palsy shakes a few, sad, last gray hairs,
  Where youth grows pale, and specter-thin, and dies,
    Where but to think is to be full of sorrow
      And leaden-eyed despairs,
  Where Beauty cannot keep her lustrous eyes,
    Or new Love pine at them beyond tomorrow.

4

Away! away! for I will fly to thee,
  Not charioted by Bacchus and his pards,
But on the viewless wings of Poesy,
  Though the dull brain perplexes and retards:
Already with thee! tender is the night,
  And haply the Queen-Moon is on her throne,
    Clustered around by all her starry Fays;
      But here there is no light,
  Save what from heaven is with the breezes blown
    Through verdurous glooms and winding mossy ways.

5

I cannot see what flowers are at my feet,
  Nor what soft incense hangs upon the boughs,
But, in embalméd darkness, guess each sweet
  Wherewith the seasonable month endows
The grass, the thicket, and the fruit tree wild;
  White hawthorn, and the pastoral eglantine;
    Fast fading violets covered up in leaves;
      And mid-May's eldest child,
  The coming musk-rose, full of dewy wine,
    The murmurous haunt of flies on summer eves.

6

Darkling I listen; and for many a time
  I have been half in love with easeful Death,
Called him soft names in many a muséd rhyme,
  To take into the air my quiet breath;
Now more than ever seems it rich to die,
  To cease upon the midnight with no pain,
    While thou art pouring forth thy soul abroad
      In such an ecstasy!
  Still wouldst thou sing, and I have ears in vain –
    To thy high requiem become a sod.

7

Thou wast not born for death, immortal Bird!
  No hungry generations tread thee down;
The voice I hear this passing night was heard
  In ancient days by emperor and clown:
Perhaps the selfsame song that found a path
  Through the sad heart of Ruth, when, sick for home,
    She stood in tears amid the alien corn;
      The same that ofttimes hath
  Charmed magic casements, opening on the foam
    Of perilous seas, in faery lands forlorn.

177

8

Forlorn! the very word is like a bell
  To toll me back from thee to my sole self!
Adieu! the fancy cannot cheat so well
  As she is famed to do, deceiving elf.
Adieu! adieu! thy plaintive anthem fades
    Past the near meadows, over the still stream,
      Up the hill side; and now 'tis buried deep
        In the next valley-glades:
    Was it a vision, or a waking dream?
      Fled is that music: – Do I wake or sleep?

STEVIE SMITH
1902–1971

Not Waving but Drowning

Nobody heard him, the dead man,
But still he lay moaning:
I was much further out than you thought
And not waving but drowning.

Poor chap, he always loved larking
And now he's dead
It must have been too cold for him his heart gave way,
They said.

Oh, no no no, it was too cold always
(Still the dead one lay moaning)
I was much too far out all my life
And not waving but drowning.

Smith spent much of her life working for a publishing company and living in Palmers Green in London. Her poetry reflects her interest in zany humour, religion, loneliness and the fear of death. She wrote in a clear, child-like style which often recalls the rhythm of nursery rhymes.

179

HENRY REED
b. 1914–1986

Lines from Lessons of the War

1. Naming of Parts
Today we have naming of parts. Yesterday,
We had daily cleaning. And tomorrow morning,
We shall have what to do after firing. But today,
Today, we have naming of parts. Japonica
Glistens like coral in all of the neighbouring gardens,
    And today we have naming of parts.

This is the lower sling swivel. And this
Is the upper sling swivel, whose use you will see,
When you are given your slings. And this is the piling swivel,
Which in your case you have not got. The branches
Hold in the gardens their silent, eloquent gestures,
    Which in our case we have not got.

This is the safety-catch, which is always released
With an easy flick of the thumb. And please do not let me
See anyone using his finger. You can do it quite easy
If you have any strength in your thumb. The blossoms
Are fragile and motionless, never letting anyone see
    Any of them using their finger.

And this you can see is the bolt. The purpose of this
Is to open the breech, as you see. We can slide it
Rapidly backwards and forwards: we call this
Easing the spring. And rapidly backwards and forwards
The early bees are assaulting and fumbling the flowers:
    They call it easing the Spring.

They call it easing the Spring: it is perfectly easy
If you have any strength in your thumb: like the bolt,
And the breech, and the cocking-piece, and the point of balance,
Which in our case we have not got; and the almond-blossom
Silent in all of the gardens and the bees going backwards and forwards,
  For today we have naming of parts.

Reed's mother could neither read nor write but she had an exceptional memory. She was always telling stories and this encouraged Reed's love of literature. As an adult he worked as a teacher and a writer. He researched a biography of the novelist and poet Thomas Hardy but it was never completed and he began to concentrate on writing plays for radio instead.

This poem, on the subject of learning to use a gun, is Reed's most famous work. It was written during the Second World War, in 1942. The central character in the poem is hovering at the edge of a weapon training squad. He is half listening to the words of his instructor but his attention keeps wandering as he observes the natural world around him. The poem emphasizes the contrast between the violence of death and the beauty and renewal in the world of the living.

IRINA RATUSHINSKAYA
b. 1954

No, I'm Not Afraid

No, I'm not afraid: after a year
Of breathing these prison nights
I will survive into the sadness
To name which is escape.

The cockerel will weep freedom for me
And here − knee-deep in mire −
My gardens shed their water
And the northern air blows in draughts.

And how am I to carry to an alien planet
What are almost tears, as though towards home . . .
It isn't true, I *am* afraid, my darling!
But make it look as though you haven't noticed.

(trans. David McDuff)

CRAIG RAINE
b. 1944

A Martian Sends a Postcard Home

Caxtons are mechanical birds with many wings
and some are treasured for their markings –

they cause the eyes to melt
or the body to shriek without pain.

I have never seen one fly, but
sometimes they perch on the hand.

Mist is when the sky is tired of flight
and rests its soft machine on ground:

then the world is dim and bookish
like engravings under tissue paper.

Rain is when the earth is television.
It has the property of making colours darker.

Model T is a room with the lock inside –
a key is turned to free the world

for movement, so quick there is a film
to watch for anything missed.

But time is tied to the wrist
or kept in a box, ticking with impatience.

In homes, a haunted apparatus sleeps,
that snores when you pick it up.

If the ghost cries, they carry it
to their lips and soothe it to sleep

with sounds. And yet, they wake it up
deliberately, by tickling with a finger.

Only the young are allowed to suffer
openly. Adults go to a punishment room

with water but nothing to eat.
They lock the door and suffer the noises

alone. No one is exempt
and everyone's pain has a different smell.

At night, when all the colours die,
they hide in pairs

and read about themselves –
in colour, with their eyelids shut.

———

Raine lives in Oxford. He has become associated with the 'Martian School of Poetry'. This is a joke name for poets who are interested in pretending to be outsiders and observing the world around them as aliens looking at it for the first time. This method of writing encourages us to notice things about our everyday lives which may otherwise go unnoticed.

WILFRED OWEN
1893–1918

Anthem for Doomed Youth

What passing-bells for these who die as cattle?
   Only the monstrous anger of the guns.
   Only the stuttering rifles' rapid rattle
Can patter out their hasty orisons.
No mockeries now for them; no prayers nor bells,
   Nor any voice of mourning save the choirs –
The shrill, demented choirs of wailing shells;
   And bugles calling for them from sad shires.

What candles may be held to speed them all?
   Not in the hands of boys, but in their eyes
Shall shine the holy glimmers of good-byes.
   The pallor of girls' brows shall be their pall;
Their flowers the tenderness of patient minds,
And each slow dusk a drawing-down of blinds.

BENJAMIN ZEPHANIAH
b. 1958

It's Work

I could hav been a builder
A painter or a swimmer
I dreamt of being a Rasta writer,
I fancied me a farmer
I could never be a barber
Once I was not sure about de future,
Got a sentence an I done it
Still me angry feelings groweth
Now I am jus a different fighter,
I sight de struggle up more clearly
I get younger yearly
An me black heart don't get no lighter.
I will not join de army
I would work wid malt an barley
But here I am checking me roots,
I could work de ital kitchen
But I won't cook dead chicken
An I won't lick nobody's boots,
Yes I could be a beggar
Maybe not a tax collector
I could be a streetwise snob,
But I'll jus keep reciting de poems dat I am writing
One day I'll hav a proper job.

WILFRED WILSON GIBSON
1878–1962

Lament

We who are left, how shall we look again
Happily on the sun or feel the rain,
Without remembering how they who went
Ungrudgingly, and spent
Their all for us, loved too the sun and rain?

A bird among the rain-wet lilac sings –
But we, how shall we turn to little things,
And listen to the birds and winds and streams
Made holy by their dreams,
Nor feel the heart-break in the heart of things?

PASTOR NIEMÖLLER
1892–1984

First They Came for the Jews

First they came for the Jews
and I did not speak out –
because I was not a Jew.
Then they came for the communists
and I did not speak out –
because I was not a communist.
Then they came for the trade unionists
and I did not speak out –
because I was not a trade unionist.
Then they came for me –
and there was no one left
to speak out for me.

The Reverend Martin Niemöller was a Lutheran minister who opposed the Nazis in Germany in the 1930s. Many other church ministers chose silence and failed to speak out against the horrendous persecution of the Jews.

189

ANDREW BARTON 'BANJO' PATERSON
1864–1941

The Man from Snowy River

There was movement at the station, for the word had passed around
That the colt from old Regret had got away,
And had joined the wild bush horses – he was worth a thousand pound,
So all the cracks had gathered to the fray.
All the tried and noted riders from the stations near and far
Had mustered at the homestead overnight,
For the bushmen love hard riding where the wild bush horses are,
And the stockhorse snuffs the battle with delight.

There was Harrison, who made his pile when Pardon won the cup,
The old man with his hair as white as snow;
But few could ride beside him when his blood was fairly up –
He would go wherever horse and man could go.
And Clancy of the Overflow came down to lend a hand,
No better horseman ever held the reins;
For never horse could throw him while the saddle girths would stand,
He learnt to ride while droving on the plains.

And one was there, a stripling on a small and weedy beast,
He was something like a racehorse undersized,
With a touch of Timor pony – three parts thoroughbred at least –
And such as are by mountain horsemen prized.
He was hard and tough and wiry – just the sort that won't say die –
There was courage in his quick impatient tread;
And he bore the badge of gameness in his bright and fiery eye,
And the proud and lofty carriage of his head.

But still so slight and weedy, one would doubt his power to stay,
And the old man said, 'That horse will never do
For a long and tiring gallop – lad, you'd better stop away,
Those hills are far too rough for such as you.'
So he waited sad and wistful – only Clancy stood his friend –
'I think we ought to let him come,' he said;
'I warrant he'll be with us when he's wanted at the end,
For both his horse and he are mountain bred.

'He hails from Snowy River, up by Kosciusko's side,
Where the hills are twice as steep and twice as rough,
Where a horse's hoofs strike firelight from the flint stones every stride,
The man that holds his own is good enough.
And the Snowy River riders on the mountains make their home,
Where the river runs those giant hills between;
I have seen full many horsemen since I first commenced to roam,
But nowhere yet such horsemen have I seen.'

So he went – they found the horses by the big mimosa clump –
They raced away towards the mountain's brow,
And the old man gave his orders, 'Boys, go at them from the jump,
No use to try for fancy riding now.
And, Clancy, you must wheel them, try and wheel them to the right.
Ride boldly, lad, and never fear the spills,
For never yet was rider that could keep the mob in sight,
If once they gain the shelter of those hills.'

So Clancy rode to wheel them – he was racing on the wing
Where the best and boldest riders take their place,
And he raced his stockhorse past them, and he made the ranges ring
With the stockwhip, as he met them face to face.
Then they halted for a moment, while he swung the dreaded lash,
But they saw their well-loved mountain full in view,
And they charged beneath the stockwhip with a sharp and sudden dash,
And off into the mountain scrub they flew.

Then fast the horsemen followed, where the gorges deep and black
Resounded to the thunder of their tread,
And the stockwhips woke the echoes, and they fiercely answered back
From cliffs and crags that beetled overhead.
And upward, ever upward, the wild horses held their way,
Where mountain ash and kurrajong grew wide;
And the old man muttered fiercely, 'We may bid the mob good day,
No man can hold them down the other side.'

When they reached the mountain's summit, even Clancy took a pull,
It well might make the boldest hold their breath,
The wild hop scrub grew thickly, and the hidden ground was full
Of wombat holes, and any slip was death.
But the man from Snowy River let the pony have his head,
And he swung his stockwhip round and gave a cheer,
And he raced him down the mountain like a torrent down its bed,
While the others stood and watched in very fear.

He sent the flint stones flying, but the pony kept his feet,
He cleared the fallen timber in his stride,
And the man from Snowy River never shifted in his seat –
It was grand to see that mountain horseman ride.

Through the stringybarks and saplings, on the rough and broken ground,
Down the hillside at a racing pace he went;
And he never drew the bridle till he landed safe and sound,
At the bottom of that terrible descent.

He was right among the horses as they climbed the further hill,
And the watchers on the mountain standing mute,
Saw him ply the stockwhip fiercely, he was right among them still,
As he raced across the clearing in pursuit.
Then they lost him for a moment, where two mountain gullies met
In the ranges, but a final glimpse reveals
On a dim and distant hillside the wild horses racing yet,
With the man from Snowy River at their heels.

And he ran them single-handed till their sides were white with foam.
He followed like a bloodhound on their track,
Till they halted cowed and beaten, then he turned their heads for home,
And alone and unassisted brought them back.
But his hardy mountain pony he could scarcely raise a trot,
He was blood from hip to shoulder from the spur;
But his pluck was still undaunted, and his courage fiery hot,
For never yet was mountain horse a cur.

And down by Kosciusko, where the pine-clad ridges raise
Their torn and rugged battlements on high,
Where the air is clear as crystal, and the white stars fairly blaze
At midnight in the cold and frosty sky,
And where around The Overflow the reed beds sweep and sway
To the breezes, and the rolling plains are wide,
The man from Snowy River is a household word today,
And the stockmen tell the story of his ride.

Paterson published his poetry under the pen name 'Banjo'. From the late nineteenth century until about 1930 ballads were very popular in Australia. His most famous lyrics are those for the Australian national song 'Waltzing Matilda'. He also worked as a solicitor and as a war correspondent for newspapers during the Boer War.

OGDEN NASH
1902–1971

The Duck

Behold the duck.
It does not cluck.
A cluck it lacks.
It quacks.
It is specially fond
Of a puddle or pond.
When it dines or sups,
It bottoms ups.

Ogden Nash was born in New York, worked in advertising and later as a screenwriter in Hollywood. He first tried to write serious poetry but considered his efforts clumsy and sentimental. When he turned to comic verses, they proved a big hit with an audience fed up with complicated poetry. Nash's rhymes suggest that even when life might seem disastrous, it's not always so bad.

MARIANNE MOORE
1887–1972

The Steeple-Jack

Dürer would have seen a reason for living
    in a town like this, with eight stranded whales
to look at; with the sweet sea air coming into your house
on a fine day, from water etched
    with waves as formal as the scales
on a fish.

One by one in two's and three's, the seagulls keep
    flying back and forth over the town clock,
or sailing around the lighthouse without moving their wings –
rising steadily with a slight
    quiver of the body – or flock
mewing where

a sea the purple of the peacock's neck is
    paled to greenish azure as Dürer changed
the pine green of the Tyrol to peacock blue and guinea
gray. You can see a twenty-five-
    pound lobster; and fishnets arranged
to dry. The

whirlwind fife-and-drum of the storm bends the salt
    marsh grass, disturbs stars in the sky and the
star on the steeple; it is a privilege to see so
much confusion. Disguised by what
    might seem the opposite, the sea-
side flowers and

trees are favored by the fog so that you have
    the tropics at first hand: the trumpet-vine,
fox-glove, giant snap-dragon, a salpiglossis that has
spots and stripes; morning-glories, gourds,
    or moon-vines trained on fishing-twine
at the back

door; cat-tails, flags, blueberries and spiderwort,
     striped grass, lichens, sunflowers asters, daisies –
yellow and crab-claw ragged sailors with green bracts – toad-plant,
petunias, ferns; pink lilies, blue
     ones, tigers; poppies; black sweet-peas.
The climate

is not right for the banyan, frangipani, or
     jack-fruit trees; or an exotic serpent
life. Ring lizard and snake-skin for the foot, if you see fit;
but here they've cats, not cobras, to
     keep down the rats. The diffident
little newt

with white pin-dots on black horizontal spaced
     out bands lives here; yet there is nothing that
ambition can buy or take away. The college student
named Ambrose sits on the hillside
     with his not-native books and hat
and sees boats

at sea progress white and rigid as if in
     a groove. Liking an elegance of which
the source is not bravado, he knows by heart the antique
sugar-bowl shaped summer-house of
     interlacing slats, and the pitch
of the church

spire, not true, from which a man in scarlet lets
     down a rope as a spider spins a thread;
he might be part of a novel, but on the sidewalk a
sign says C.J. Poole, Steeple Jack,
     in black and white; and one in red
and white says

Danger. The church portico has four fluted
     columns, each a single piece of stone, made
modester by white-wash. This would be a fit haven for
waifs, children, animals, prisoners,
     and presidents who have repaid
sin-driven

senators by not thinking about them. The
     place has a school-house, a post-office in a
store, fish-houses, hen-houses, a three-masted
     schooner on
the stocks. The hero, the student,
     the steeple-jack, each in his way,
is at home.

It could not be dangerous to be living
    in a town like this, of simple people,
who have a steeple-jack placing danger-signs by the church
while he is gilding the solid-
    pointed star, which on a steeple
stands for hope.

———————

Born in Missouri, in the United States, Marianne Moore worked in universities and as an editor but she was also a dedicated baseball fan and loved to make sketches from nature. She admitted that she sometimes found poetry boring but at other times, when she found a poem that she really loved, she realized how enjoyable it could be.

CHARLES KINGSLEY
1819—1875

Young and Old

When all the world is young, lad,
  And all the trees are green;
And every goose a swan, lad,
  And every lass a queen;
Then hey for boot and horse, lad,
  And round the world away;
Young blood must have its course, lad,
  And every dog his day.

When all the world is old, lad,
  And all the trees are brown;
And all the sport is stale, lad,
  And all the wheels run down;
Creep home, and take your place there,
  The spent and maimed among:
God grant you find one face there,
  You loved when all was young.

PHILIP LARKIN
1922–1985

Days

What are days for?
Days are where we live.
They come, they wake us
Time and time over.

They are to be happy in:
Where can we live but days?

Ah, solving that question
Brings the priest and the doctor
In their long coats
Running over the fields.

For most of his life Philip Larkin worked as a librarian. As a young man he was influenced by William Butler Yeats but he later came to believe that such poetry was too dramatic. He wrote his own very slowly and paid a great deal of attention to detail. This meant that it took him a long time to finish most of his poems, and consequently his published output was not great. Despite this, he was one of the most popular English poets of his generation. Larkin was a precise and witty observer of human behaviour and was intrigued by social conventions.

JOHN MASEFIELD
1878–1967

Sea Fever

I must go down to the seas again, to the lonely sea and the sky,
And all I ask is a tall ship and a star to steer her by;
And the wheel's kick and the wind's song and the white sail's shaking,
And a grey mist on the sea's face, and a grey dawn breaking.

I must go down to the seas again, for the call of the running tide
Is a wild call and a clear call that may not be denied;
And all I ask is a windy day with the white clouds flying,
And the flung spray and the blown spume, and the sea-gulls crying.

I must go down to the seas again, to the vagrant gypsy life,
To the gull's way and the whale's way where the wind's like a whetted
 knife;
And all I ask is a merry yarn from a laughing fellow-rover,
And quiet sleep and a sweet dream when the long trick's over.

STEVIE SMITH
1902–1971

The Sea Widow

Q.   How fares it with you, Mrs Cooper my bride?

A.   Long are the years since you lay by my side

Q.   Do you wish I was back? Do you speak of me dearest?

A.   I wish you were back for me to hold nearest

Q.   Who then lies nearer Mrs Cooper my Bride?

A.   A black man comes in on the evening tide.

Q.   What is his name? Tell me! How does he dare?

A.   He comes uninvited. His name is Despair.

WALTER DE LA MARE
1873–1956

The Listeners

'Is there anybody there?' said the Traveller,
　　Knocking on the moonlit door;
And his horse in the silence champed the grasses
　　Of the forest's ferny floor:
And a bird flew up out of the turret,
　　Above the Traveller's head:
And he smote upon the door again a second time;
　　'Is there anybody there?' he said.
But no one descended to the Traveller;
　　No head from the leaf-fringed sill
Leaned over and looked into his grey eyes,
　　Where he stood perplexed and still.
But only a host of phantom listeners
　　That dwelt in the lone house then
Stood listening in the quiet of the moonlight
　　To that voice from the world of men:
Stood thronging the faint moonbeams on the dark stair,
　　That goes down to the empty hall,
Hearkening in an air stirred and shaken
　　By the lonely Traveller's call.
And he felt in his heart their strangeness,
　　Their stillness answering his cry,
While his horse moved, cropping the dark turf,
　　'Neath the starred and leafy sky;
For he suddenly smote on the door, even
　　Louder, and lifted his head: –
'Tell them I came, and no one answered.
　　That I kept my word,' he said.
Never the least stir made the listeners,
　　Though every word he spake
Fell echoing through the shadowiness of the still house
　　From the one man left awake:
Ay, they heard his foot upon the stirrup,
　　And the sound of iron on stone,
And how the silence surged softly backward,
　　When the plunging hoofs were gone.

202

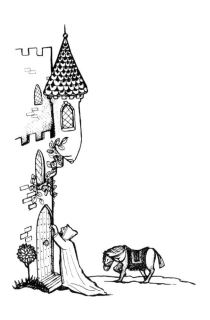

Walter De La Mare was a popular children's poet who was interested in dreams and the Supernatural and often referred to 'looking' and 'wondering' in his writing. He liked to suggest that things were not always as they first appear. He encourages us to observe the world carefully and to look beyond the merely superficial.

First published in 1912, this is De La Mare's most famous poem. It is a mysterious, atmospheric account of a traveller who is thwarted in his attempts to relay a message. We are not told why the traveller has made his journey or why 'the listeners' won't open the door to him. Even the title of the poem is ambiguous: 'the listeners' might be aware of their visitor but they do not welcome him or listen to what he has to say.

EDWIN MUIR
1887–1959

Scotland's Winter

Now the ice lays its smooth claws on the sill,
The sun looks from the hill
Helmed in his winter casket,
And sweeps his arctic sword across the sky.
The water at the mill
Sounds more hoarse and dull.
The miller's daughter walking by
With frozen fingers soldered to her basket
Seems to be knocking
Upon a hundred leagues of floor
With her light heels, and mocking
Percy and Douglas dead,
And Bruce on his burial bed,
Where he lies white as may
With wars and leprosy,
And all the kings before
This land was kingless,
And all the singers before
This land was songless.
This land that with its dead and living waits the Judgment Day.
But they, the powerless dead,
Listening can hear no more
Than a hard tapping on the sounding floor
A little overhead
Of common heels that do not know
Whence they come or where they go
And are content
With their poor frozen life and shallow banishment.

Muir came from the Orkney islands. He had many jobs in his life, including a position in a beer bottling factory in Glasgow. He also worked as a translator and when he wrote about nature he tried to see it with all the vividness that he had seen as a child. He thought that we should try to understand all living things and respect the differences between them and us.

DENISE LEVERTOV
b. 1923

Scenes from the Life of the Peppertrees

1
The peppertrees, the peppertrees!

Cats are stretching in the doorways,
sure of everything. It is morning.
    But the peppertrees
stand aside in diffidence, with berries
of modest red.
            Branch above branch, an air
of lightness; of shadows
scattered lightly.
            A cat
closes upon its shadow.
Up and up goes the sun,
sure of everything.
        The peppertrees
            shiver a little.
Robust
and soot-black, the cat
leaps to a low branch. Leaves
close about him.

2
The yellow moon dreamily
tipping buttons of light
down among the leaves. Marimba,
marimba – from beyond the
black street.
            Somebody dancing,
somebody
            getting the hell
outta here. Shadows of cats
weave round the tree trunks.
the exposed knotty roots.

3

The man on the bed sleeping
defenseless. Look –
his bare long feet together
sideways, keeping each other
warm. And the foreshortened shoulders,
the head
barely visible   He is good.
let him sleep.
                    But the third peppertree
        is restless, twitching
thin leaves in the light
of afternoon. After a while
it walks over and taps
on the upstairs window with a bunch
of red berries. Will he wake?

Levertov was born in England. Her mother was Welsh, her father was a Russian Jew and her family home became a refuge for Jews escaping Nazism. Her first collection of poetry was published in 1946 and in 1948 she emigrated to the United States. She became a committed campaigner for women's rights. Much of her poetry, which was deeply influenced by William Carlos Williams, reflects her political concerns, although others acknowledge and pay homage to the power of nature.

RUDYARD KIPLING
1865–1936

Mandalay

By the old Moulmein Pagoda, lookin' eastward to the sea,
There's a Burma girl a-settin', an' I know she thinks o' me;
For the wind is in the palm-trees, an' the temple-bells they say:
'Come you back, you British soldier; come you back to
　　Mandalay!'
　　Come you back to Mandalay,
　　Where the old Flotilla lay:
　　Can't you 'ear their paddles chunkin' from Rangoon to
　　　　Mandalay?
　　On the road to Mandalay,
　　Where the flyin'-fishes play,
　　An' the dawn comes up like thunder outer China 'crost the Bay!

'Er petticut was yaller an' 'er little cap was green,
An' 'er name was Supi-yaw-let – jes' the same as Theebaw's
   Queen,
An' I seed her fust a-smokin' of a whackin' white cheroot,
An' a-wastin' Christian kisses on an 'eathen idol's foot:
     Bloomin' idol made o' mud –
     What they called the Great Gawd Budd –
     Plucky lot she cared for idols when I kissed 'er where she
      stud!
     On the road to Mandalay –

When the mist was on the rice-fields an' the sun was droppin'
   slow,
She'd git 'er little banjo an' she'd sing '*Kulla-lo-lo!*'
With 'er arm upon my shoulder an' her cheek agin my cheek
We useter watch the steamers, an' the *hathis* pilin' teak.
     Elephints a-pilin' teak
     In the sludgy, squdgy creek,
     Where the silence 'ung that 'eavy you was 'arf afraid to
      speak!
     On the road to Mandalay –

But that's all shove be'ind me – long ago an' fur away,
An' there ain't no 'busses runnin' from the Bank to Mandalay;
An' I'm learnin' 'ere in London what the ten-year sodger tells:
'If you've 'eard the East a-callin', why, you won't 'eed nothin'
   else.'
     No! you won't 'eed nothin' else
     But them spicy garlic smells
     An' the sunshine an' the palm-trees an' the tinkly temple
      bells!
     On the road to Mandalay –

I am sick o' wastin' leather on these gritty pavin'-stones,
An' the blasted Henglish drizzle wakes the fever in my bones;
Tho' I walks with fifty 'ousemaids outer Chelsea to the Strand,
An' they talks a lot o' lovin', but wot do they understand?
     Beefy face an' grubby 'and –
     Law! wot *do* they understand?
     I've a neater, sweeter maiden in a cleaner, greener land!
     On the road to Mandalay –

Ship me somewheres east of Suez where the best is like the worst,
Where there aren't no Ten Commandments, an' a man can raise
   a thirst;
For the temple-bells are callin' an' it's there that I would be –
By the old Moulmein Pagoda, lookin' lazy at the sea –
       On the road to Mandalay,
       Where the old Flotilla lay,
       With our sick beneath the awnings when we went to
         Mandalay!
       Oh, the road to Mandalay,
       Where the flyin' fishes play,
       An' the dawn comes up like thunder outer China 'crost
         the Bay!

WOLE SOYINKA
b. 1934

Night

Your hand is heavy, Night, upon my brow,
I bear no heart mercuric like the clouds, to dare
Exacerbation from your subtle plough.

Woman as a clam, on the sea's crescent
I saw your jealous eye quench the sea's
Fluorescence, dance on the pulse incessant

Of the waves. And I stood, drained
Submitting like the sands, blood and brine
Coursing to the roots. Night, you rained

Serrated shadows through dank leaves
Till, bathed in warm suffusion of your dappled cells
Sensations pained me, faceless, silent as night thieves.

Hide me now, when night children haunt the earth
I must hear none! These misted calls will yet
Undo me; naked, unbidden, at Night's muted birth.

TED HUGHES
1930–1999

The Thought Fox

I imagine this midnight moment's forest:
Something else is alive
Beside the clock's loneliness
And this blank page where my fingers move.

Through the window I see no star:
Something more near
Though deeper within darkness
Is entering the loneliness:

Cold, delicately as the dark snow,
A fox's nose touches twig, leaf;
Two eyes serve a movement, that now
And again now, and now, and now

Sets neat prints into the snow
Between trees, and warily a lame
Shadow lags by stump and in hollow
Of a body that is bold to come

Across clearings, an eye,
A widening deepening greenness,
Brilliantly, concentratedly,
Coming about its own business

Till, with a sudden sharp hot stink of fox
It enters the dark hole of the head.
The window is starless still; the clock ticks,
The page is printed.

Ted Hughes was a rural Yorkshire man who felt that the rugged landscape of his childhood had a profound influence on his poetry. As an adult he adopted North Devon as his home and the landscape there became an inspiration too. He was first married to the poet Sylvia Plath. The language he employs in his poetry describes instinctive reactions to a subject and is frequently harsh and challenging.

This poem appeared in Hughes' first published collection The Hawk in the Rain *in 1957. It compares the experience of trying to write, trying to make sense of the ideas that come into our minds, with a fox prowling through the darkness and coming to the foreground 'with a sudden hot sharp stink'.*

PHILIP LARKIN
1922–1985

Toads

Why should I let the toad *work*
   Squat on my life?
Can't I use my wit as a pitchfork
   And drive the brute off?

Six days of the week it soils
   With its sickening poison –
Just for paying a few bills!
   That's out of proportion.

Lots of folk live on their wits:
   Lecturers, lispers,
Losels, loblolly-men, louts –
   They don't end as paupers;

Lots of folk live up lanes
   With fires in a bucket,
Eat windfalls and tinned sardines –
   They seem to like it.

Their nippers have got bare feet,
   Their unspeakable wives
Are skinny as whippets – and yet
   No one actually *starves*.

Ah, were I courageous enough
   To shout *Stuff your pension!*
But I know, all too well, that's the stuff
   That dreams are made on:

For something sufficiently toad-like
   Squats in me, too;
Its hunkers are heavy as hard luck,
   And cold as snow,

And will never allow me to blarney
   My way to getting
The fame and the girl and the money
   All at one sitting.

I don't say, one bodies the other
   One's spiritual truth;
But I do say it's hard to lose either,
   When you have both.

THOMAS HARDY
1840–1928

The Voice

Woman much missed, how you call to me, call to me,
Saying that now you are not as you were
When you had changed from the one who was all to me,
But as at first, when our day was fair.

Can it be you that I hear? Let me view you, then,
Standing as when I drew near to the town
Where you would wait for me: yes, as I knew you then,
Even to the original air-blue gown!

Or is it only the breeze, in its listlessness
Travelling across the wet mead to me here,
You being ever dissolved to wan wistlessness,
Heard no more again far or near?

Thus I; faltering forward,
Leaves around me falling,
Wind oozing thin through the thorn from norward,
And the woman calling.

Hardy was born in Dorset and trained as an architect. He is best known for famous novels like Tess of the D'Urbervilles *and* Jude the Obscure. *In later life he concentrated on poetry inspired by tragic stories from everyday life. He lost his Christian faith but believed that man had ultimately no power over the natural world. His poems often deal with a sense of loss and regret.*

Hardy's wife died in 1912, the year this poem was written. He felt guilty that he had neglected her in the last years of her life and wrote over fifty poems recalling their earlier love.

216

SIR JOHN BETJEMAN
1906–1984

A Subaltern's Love-song

Miss J. Hunter Dunn, Miss J. Hunter Dunn,
Furnish'd and burnish'd by Aldershot sun,
What strenuous singles we played after tea,
We in the tournament – you against me!

Love-thirty, love-forty, oh! weakness of joy,
The speed of a swallow, the grace of a boy,
With carefullest carelessness, gaily you won,
I am weak from your loveliness, Joan Hunter Dunn.

Miss Joan Hunter Dunn, Miss Joan Hunter Dunn,
How mad I am, sad I am, glad that you won.
The warm-handled racket is back in its press,
But my shock-headed victor, she loves me no less.

Her father's euonymus shines as we walk,
And swing past the summer-house, buried in talk,
And cool the verandah that welcomes us in
To the six-o'clock news and a lime-juice and gin.

The scent of the conifers, sound of the bath,
The view from my bedroom of moss-dappled path,
As I struggle with double-end evening tie,
For we dance at the Golf Club, my victor and I.

On the floor of her bedroom lie blazer and shorts
And the cream-coloured walls are be-trophied with sports,
And westering, questioning settles the sun
On your low-leaded window, Miss Joan Hunter Dunn.

The Hillman is waiting, the light's in the hall,
The pictures of Egypt are bright on the wall,
My sweet, I am standing beside the oak stair
And there on the landing's the light on your hair.

By roads 'not adopted', by woodlanded ways,
She drove to the club in the late summer haze,
Into nine-o'clock Camberley, heavy with bells
And mushroomy, pine-woody, evergreen smells.

Miss Joan Hunter Dunn, Miss Joan Hunter Dunn,
I can hear from the car-park the dance has begun.
Oh! full Surrey twilight! importunate band!
Oh! strongly adorable tennis-girl's hand!

Around us are Rovers and Austins afar,
Above us, the intimate roof of the car,
And here on my right is the girl of my choice,
With the tilt of her nose and the chime of her voice,

And the scent of her wrap, and the words never said,
And the ominous, ominous dancing ahead.
We sat in the car-park till twenty to one
And now I'm engaged to Miss Joan Hunter Dunn.

———————————

Betjeman is famous for poems that make fun of the English. His poetry is affectionately mocking. His subject matter was often suburbia, the sea, his childhood fears and later love affairs. He also wrote books on architecture and was a popular presenter of television documentaries. He had a hearty laugh and usually wore a slightly squashed hat.

This is one of Betjeman's best known poems. It describes the experience of falling in love with a girl with whom he played tennis. As the story unfolds, Betjeman's relationship with Joan Hunter Dunn clearly becomes less and less formal. It celebrates the couples' engagement but in typical Betjeman style, gently pokes fun at the English reserve and at their nostalgic home comforts.

IBARAGI NORIKO
b. 1926

When I Was Prettiest in my Life

When I was prettiest in my life,
the cities crumbled down,
and the blue sky appeared
in the most unexpected places.

When I was prettiest in my life,
a lot of people around me were killed,
in factories, in the sea, and on nameless islands.
I lost the chance to dress up like a girl should.

When I was prettiest in my life,
no men offered me thoughtful gifts.
They only knew how to salute in the military fashion.
They all went off to the front, leaving their beautiful eyes behind.

When I was prettiest in my life,
my head was empty,
my heart was obstinate,
and only my limbs had the bright colour of chestnuts.

When I was prettiest in my life,
my country lost in a war.
'How can it be true?' I asked,
striding, with my sleeves rolled up, through the prideless town.

When I was prettiest in my life,
jazz music streamed from the radio.
Feeling dizzy, as if I'd broken a resolve to quit smoking,
I devoured the sweet music of a foreign land.

When I was prettiest in my life,
I was most unhappy,
I was most absurd,
I was helplessly lonely.

Therefore I decided to live a long time, if I could,
like old Rouault of France,
who painted magnificent pictures in his old age.

(trans. Naoshi Koriyama and Edward Lueders)

DEREK WALCOTT
b. 1930

A Far Cry from Africa

A wind is ruffling the tawny pelt
Of Africa. Kikuyu, quick as flies,
Batten upon the bloodstreams of the veldt.
Corpses are scattered through a paradise.
Only the worm, colonel of carrion, cries:
'Waste no compassion on these separate dead!'
Statistics justify and scholars seize
The salients of colonial policy.
What is that to the white child hacked in bed?
To savages, expendable as Jews?

Threshed out by beaters, the long rushes break
In a white dust of ibises whose cries
Have wheeled since civilization's dawn
From the parched river or beast-teeming plain.
The violence of beast on beast is read
As natural law, but upright man
Seeks his divinity by inflicting pain.
Delirious as these worried beasts, his wars
Dance to the tightened carcass of a drum,
While he calls courage still that native dread
Of the white peace contracted by the dead.

Again brutish necessity wipes its hands
Upon the napkin of a dirty cause, again
A waste of our compassion, as with Spain,
The gorilla wrestles with the superman.
I who am poisoned with the blood of both,
Where shall I turn, divided to the vein?
I who have cursed
The drunken officer of British rule, how choose
Between this Africa and the English tongue I love?
Betray them both, or give back what they give?
How can I face such slaughter and be cool?
How can I turn from Africa and live?

ROBERT FROST
1874–1963

Stopping by Woods on a Snowy Evening

Whose woods these are I think I know.
His house is in the village, though;
He will not see me stopping here
To watch his woods fill up with snow.

My little horse must think it queer
To stop without a farmhouse near
Between the woods and frozen lake
The darkest evening of the year.

He gives his harness bells a shake
To ask if there is some mistake.
The only other sound's the sweep
Of easy wind and downy flake.

The woods are lovely, dark, and deep,
But I have promises to keep,
And miles to go before I sleep,
And miles to go before I sleep.

As a young man Frost worked as a farmer in New Hampshire in the United States with his wife and six children. He did not like cities, and his poetry reflects a fondness for country life: snowy evenings, stone walls and apple picking. His work is down to earth and the rhythms are similar to conversational speech, although Frost does not attempt to conceal how confusing and destructive life can be. His own life was scarred by tragedy, including the death of several of his children.

CHRISTINA ROSSETTI
1830–1894

Echo

Come to me in the silence of the night;
  Come in the speaking silence of a dream;
Come with soft rounded cheeks and eyes as bright
    As sunlight on a stream;
      Come back in tears,
O memory, hope, love of finished years.

Oh dream how sweet, too sweet, too bitter sweet,
  Whose wakening should have been in Paradise,
Where souls brimful of love abide and meet;
    Where thirsting longing eyes
      Watch the slow door
That opening, letting in, lets out no more.

Yet come to me in dreams, that I may live
  My very life again tho' cold in death:
Come back to me in dreams, that I may give
    Pulse for pulse, breath for breath:
      Speak low, lean low,
As long ago, my love, how long ago.

W.H.AUDEN
1907–1973

Night Mail

I

This is the Night Mail crossing the Border,
Bringing the cheque and the postal order,

Letters for the rich, letters for the poor,
The shop at the corner, the girl next door.

Pulling up Beattock, a steady climb:
The gradient's against her, but she's on time.

Past cotton-grass and moorland boulder,
Shovelling white steam over her shoulder,

Snorting noisily, she passes
Silent miles of wind-bent grasses.

Birds turn their heads as she approaches,
Stare from bushes at her blank-faced coaches.

Sheep-dogs cannot turn her course;
They slumber on with paws across.

In the farm she passes no one wakes,
But a jug in a bedroom gently shakes.

II

Dawn freshens. Her climb is done.
Down towards Glasgow she descends,
Towards the steam tugs yelping down a glade of cranes,
Towards the fields of apparatus, the furnaces
Set on the dark plain like gigantic chessmen.
All Scotland waits for her:
In dark glens, beside pale-green lochs,
Men long for news.

III

Letters of thanks, letters from banks,
Letters of joy from girl and boy,
Receipted bills and invitations
To inspect new stock or to visit relations,
And applications for situations,
And timid lovers' declarations,
And gossip, gossip from all the nations,
News circumstantial, news financial,
Letters with holiday snaps to enlarge in,
Letters with faces scrawled on the margin,
Letters from uncles, cousins and aunts,
Letters to Scotland from the South of France,
Letters of condolence to Highlands and Lowlands,
Written on paper of every hue,
The pink, the violet, the white and the blue,
The chatty, the catty, the boring, the adoring,
The cold and official and the heart's outpouring,
Clever, stupid, short and long,
The typed and the printed and the spelt all wrong.

IV

Thousands are still asleep,
Dreaming of terrifying monsters
Or a friendly tea beside the band in Cranston's or Crawford's:
Asleep in working Glasgow, asleep in well-set Edinburgh,
Asleep in granite Aberdeen,
They continue their dreams,
But shall wake soon and hope for letters,
And none will hear the postman's knock
Without a quickening of the heart.
For who can bear to feel himself forgotten?

JENNY JOSEPH
b. 1932

Warning

When I am an old woman I shall wear purple
With a red hat which doesn't go, and doesn't suit me.
And I shall spend my pension on brandy and summer gloves
And satin sandals, and say we've no money for butter.
I shall sit down on the pavement when I'm tired
And gobble up samples in shops and press alarm bells
And run my stick along the public railings
And make up for the sobriety of my youth.
I shall go out in my slippers in the rain
And pick the flowers in other people's gardens
And learn to spit.

You can wear terrible shirts and grow more fat
And eat three pounds of sausages at a go
Or only bread and pickle for a week
And hoard pens and pencils and beermats and things in boxes.

But now we must have clothes that keep us dry
And pay our rent and not swear in the street
And set a good example for the children.
We must have friends to dinner and read the papers.

But maybe I ought to practise a little now?
So people who know me are not too shocked and surprised
When suddenly I am old, and start to wear purple.

Jenny Joseph is a poet, journalist and children's writer. She enjoys writing about ordinary events, like imagining the lives of people she might encounter in a shopping precinct. 'Warning' was one of her poems that Philip Larkin particularly liked.

RUDYARD KIPLING
1865–1936

If you can keep your head when all about you
    Are losing theirs and blaming it on you,
If you can trust yourself when all men doubt you,
    But make allowance for their doubting too;
If you can wait and not be tired by waiting,
    Or being lied about, don't deal in lies,
Or being hated, don't give way to hating,
    And yet don't look too good, nor talk too wise:
If you can dream – and not make dreams your master;
    If you can think – and not make thoughts your aim;
If you can meet with Triumph and Disaster
    And treat those two impostors just the same;
If you can bear to hear the truth you've spoken
    Twisted by knaves to make a trap for fools,
Or watch the things you gave your life to, broken,
    And stoop and build 'em up with worn-out tools:

If you can make one heap of all your winnings
    And risk it on one turn of pitch-and-toss,
And lose, and start again at your beginnings
    And never breathe a word about your loss;
If you can force your heart and nerve and sinew
    To serve your turn long after they are gone,
And so hold on when there is nothing in you
    Except the Will which says to them: 'Hold on!'

If you can talk with crowds and keep your virtue,
    Or walk with Kings – nor lose the common touch,
If neither foes nor loving friends can hurt you,
    If all men count with you, but none too much;
If you can fill the unforgiving minute
    With sixty seconds' worth of distance run,
Yours is the Earth and everything that's in it,
    And – which is more – you'll be a Man, my son!

The poet and popular short story writer, Kipling, was born in Bombay, India, of English parents. He is best known as a writer about India and the old British Empire and, of course, as the author of The Jungle Book. *T S Eliot was a great admirer of Kipling's writing, which is often concerned with courage, morality and 'not letting the side down'. When Kipling's own son died in the First World War his work began to question these values in a more subtle way.*

SIR HENRY NEWBOLT
1862–1938

Vitaï Lampada

There's a breathless hush in the Close to-night –
  Ten to make and the match to win –
A bumping pitch and a blinding light,
  An hour to play and the last man in.
And it's not for the sake of a ribboned coat,
  Or the selfish hope of a season's fame,
But his Captain's hand on his shoulder smote –
  'Play up! play up! and play the game!'

The sand of the desert is sodden red, –
  Red with the wreck of a square that broke; –
The Gatling's jammed and the Colonel dead,
  And the regiment blind with dust and smoke.
The river of death has brimmed his banks.
  And England's far, and Honour a name,
But the voice of a schoolboy rallies the ranks:
  'Play up! play up! and play the game!'

This is the word that year by year,
  While in her place the School is set,
Every one of her sons must hear,
  And none that hears it dare forget.
This they all with a joyful mind
  Bear through life like a torch in flame,
And falling fling to the host behind –
  'Play up! play up! and play the game!'

Newbolt was born in Staffordshire and trained as a lawyer, but he enjoyed writing and his patriotic poems achieved literary success in the late 1890s.

He sang the praises of traditional male virtues and the role of the fighting soldier.

This poem is a splendid evocation of Newbolt's 'stiff-upper-lip' approach to public life. 'Play up and play the game' became and to some extent is still a familiar instruction to schoolboys who have always been encouraged to learn this poem by heart, and to live their lives by its essential message.

LI PO
701–762

Spring Thoughts

When the grass in Yen is still jade thread,
The mulberries of Ch'in are drooping green boughs.
The days when your mind is filled with returning,
Those are the times when my heart is breaking.
But the spring wind and I have been strangers,
What is it doing in my gauze bedcurtains?

(trans. Elling O. Eide)

TU FU
712–770

A Hawk in a Painting

From white silk   a whiff of wind and frost
grey goshawk   of art extraordinary
twitching body   alert for wily hares
She glowers askance   like a gloomy Sogdian
swivel and jess   their glitter I'd unleash
and from her lofty perch   call down her power
how she would fall   upon the pack of songsters
sprinkling   blood and feathers across the plain.

(trans. David Lattimore)

JOHN BERRYMAN
1814–1972

The Ball Poem

What is the boy now, who has lost his ball,
What, what is he to do? I saw it go
Merrily bouncing, down the street, and then
Merrily over – there it is in the water!
No use to say 'O there are other balls':
An ultimate shaking grief fixes the boy
As he stands rigid, trembling, staring down
All his young days into the harbour where
His ball went. I would not intrude on him,
A dime, another ball, is worthless. Now
He senses first responsibility
In a world of possessions. People will take balls,
Balls will be lost always, little boy,
And no one buys a ball back. Money is external.
He is learning, well behind his desperate eyes,
The epistemology of loss, how to stand up
Knowing what every man must one day know
And most know many days, how to stand up
And gradually light returns to the street,
A whistle blows, the ball is out of sight,
Soon part of me will explore the deep and dark
Floor of the harbour . . . I am everywhere,
I suffer and move, my mind and my heart move
With all that move me, under the water
Or whistling, I am not a little boy.

———————————

Berryman grew up on a farm in Oklahoma, in the United States. His father committed suicide and many of Berryman's poems are concerned with the difficulties of family life and the despairing struggle of keeping a family together.

OSIP MANDELSTAM
1891–1938

Lightheartedly Take From the Palms of My Hands

Lightheartedly take from the palms of my hands
A little sun, a little honey,
As Persephone's bees commanded us.

Not to be untied, the unmoored boat;
Not to be heard, fur-shod shadows;
Not to be silenced, life's thick terrors.

Now we have only kisses,
Bristly and crisp like bees,
Which die as they fly from the hive.

They rustle in transparent thickets of night,
Their homeland thick forest of Taigetos,
Their food – honeysuckle, mint, and time.

Lightheartedly take then my uncouth present:
This simple necklace, of dead, dried bees
Who once turned honey into sun.

(trans. James Greene)

BORIS PASTERNAK
1890–1960

From *Dr Zhivago*

Winter Night

A snowstorm made the earth tremble
through its whole frame.
A candle-flame upon a table,
only a candle-flame.

Like midges swarming in the summer,
winging to a spark,
the flakes flew in a thick shimmer
to the window from the dark.

The blizzard blew. Its rime and stubble
clung to the pane.
A candle-flame upon a table,
only a candle-flame.

High up on the bright-lit ceiling
shadows were tossed:
hands cross-clasped, feet cross-leaning,
fate in a cross.

And two small shoes fell with a clatter
to the floor, useless,
and wax drops from the night-light spattered
weeping upon a dress.

And all things faded, misted, feeble,
a grey-white dream.
A candle-flame upon a table,
only a candle-flame.

The candle felt a hidden shaking
blow hot temptation:
wings raised, like an angel's, taking
a cross-like station.

All February, storm rocked the gable
and found there the same
candle-flame upon a table,
only a candle-flame.

(trans. Edwin Morgan)

DYLAN THOMAS
1914–1953

'Do not go gentle into that good night'

Do not go gentle into that good night,
Old age should burn and rave at close of day;
Rage, rage against the dying of the light.

Though wise men at their end know dark is right,
Because their words had forked no lightning they
Do not go gentle into that good night.

Good men, the last wave by, crying how bright
Their frail deeds might have danced in a green bay,
Rage, rage against the dying of the light.

Wild men who caught and sang the sun in flight,
And learn, too late, they grieved it on its way,
Do not go gentle into that good night.

Grave men, near death, who see with blinding sight
Blind eyes could blaze like meteors and be gay,
Rage, rage against the dying of the light.

And you, my father, there on the sad height,
Curse, bless, me now with your fierce tears, I pray,
Do not go gentle into that good night.
Rage, rage against the dying of the light.

Dylan Thomas was born in Swansea, Wales. He wrote poetry and plays for radio, his most famous being Under Milk Wood *which mirrors his own childhood in Wales. His poetry drew on his personal life, and in particular on the poverty and struggles of Welsh communities and, as he became increasingly alcoholic, his own fear of death.*

ROY FULLER
1912–1991

Autobiography of a Lungworm

My normal dwelling is the lungs of swine,
    My normal shape a worm,
But other dwellings, other shapes, are mine
    Within my natural term.
Dimly I see my life, of all, the sign,
    Of better lives the germ.

The pig, though I am inoffensive, coughs,
    Finding me irritant:
My eggs go with the contents of the troughs
    From mouth to excrement –
The pig thus thinks, perhaps, he forever doffs
    His niggling resident.

The eggs lie unconsidered in the dung
    Upon the farmyard floor,
Far from the scarlet and sustaining lung:
    But happily a poor
And humble denizen provides a rung
    To make ascension sure.

The earthworm eats the eggs; inside the warm
    Cylinder larvae hatch:
For years, if necessary, in this form
    I wait the lucky match
That will return me to my cherished norm,
    My ugly pelt dispatch.

Strangely, it is the pig himself becomes
    The god inside the car:
His greed devours the earthworms; so the slums
    Of his intestines are
The setting for the act when clay succumbs
    And force steers for its star.

The larvae burrow through the bowel wall
    And, having to the dregs
Drained ignominy, gain the lung's great hall.
    They change. Once more, like pegs,
Lungworms are anchored to the rise and fall
    – And start to lay their eggs.

What does this mean? The individual,
    Nature, mutation, strife?
I feel, though I am simple, still the whole
    Is complex; and that life –
A huge, doomed throbbing – has a wiry soul
    That must escape the knife.

Fuller was born in Lancashire, qualified as a solicitor and served in the Royal Navy. As a young man his poetry was influenced by Auden. His poems try to address the pain and anxiety in all our lives. He was more concerned with recording individual problems and misunderstandings than he was in writing about global problems.

EDWARD LEAR
1812–1888

The Owl and the Pussy-Cat

1

The Owl and the Pussy-cat went to sea
  In a beautiful pea-green boat,
They took some honey, and plenty of money,
  Wrapped up in a five-pound note.
The Owl looked up to the stars above,
  And sang to a small guitar,
'O lovely Pussy! O Pussy, my love.
    What a beautiful Pussy you are,
      You are,
      You are!
  What a beautiful Pussy you are!'

2

Pussy said to the Owl, 'You elegant fowl!
  How charmingly sweet you sing!
O let us be married! too long we have tarried:
  But what shall we do for a ring?'

They sailed away, for a year and a day,
  To the land where the Bong-tree grows
And there in a wood a Piggy-wig stood
  With a ring at the end of his nose,
    His nose,
    His nose,
  With a ring at the end of his nose.

3

'Dear Pig, are you willing to sell for one shilling
  Your ring?' Said the Piggy, 'I will.'
So they took it away, and were married next day
  By the Turkey who lives on the hill.
They dined on mince, and slices of quince,
  Which they ate with a runcible spoon;
And hand in hand, on the edge of the sand
  They danced by the light of the moon,
    The moon,
    The moon,
  They danced by the light of the moon.

Lear wrote this rhyme for a little girl called Janet, the daughter of his friend John Addington Symonds. She was ill in bed and needed cheering up. The rhyme makes fun of Victorian Romantic ballads. Lear loved drawing birds and was happy to sketch an owl to illustrate his rhyme. He also loved cats and in real life had a pet striped cat with no tail, called Foss.

A.E. HOUSMAN
1859–1936

Last Poems

XL

Tell me not here, it needs not saying,
  What tune the enchantress plays
In aftermaths of soft September
  Or under blanching mays,
For she and I were long acquainted
  And I knew all her ways.

On russet floors, by waters idle,
  The pine lets fall its cone;
The cuckoo shouts all day at nothing
  In leafy dells alone;
And traveller's joy beguiles in autumn
  Hearts that have lost their own.

On acres of the seeded grasses
  The changing burnish heaves;
Or marshalled under moons of harvest
  Stand still all night the sheaves;
Or beeches strip in storms for winter
  And stain the wind with leaves.

Possess, as I possessed a season,
  The countries I resign,
Where over elmy plains the highway
  Would mount the hills and shine,
And full of shade the pillared forest
  Would murmur and be mine.

For nature, heartless, witless nature,
  Will neither care nor know
What stranger's feet may find the meadow
  And trespass there and go,
Nor ask amid the dews of morning
  If they are mine or no.

Housman was a classics professor, whose most famous poem 'The Shropshire Lad' tells a stoical and gloomy tale of young men betrayed in love. He was a keen observer of the rural landscape, but the fact that the natural world could grow in abundance, while he suffered the rejection of lost love, re-enforced his own feelings of loneliness.

JOHN KEATS
1795–1821

To Autumn

1

Season of mists and mellow fruitfulness,
  Close bosom-friend of the maturing sun;
Conspiring with him how to load and bless
  With fruit the vines that round the thatch-eaves run;
To bend with apples the mossed cottage-trees,
  And fill all fruit with ripeness to the core;
    To swell the gourd, and plump the hazel shells
  With a sweet kernel; to set budding more,
And still more, later flowers for the bees,
Until they think warm days will never cease,
    For Summer has o'er-brimmed their clammy cells.

2

Who hath not seen thee oft amid thy store?
  Sometimes whoever seeks abroad may find
Thee sitting careless on a granary floor,
  Thy hair soft-lifted by the winnowing wind;
Or on a half-reaped furrow sound asleep,
  Drowsed with the fume of poppies, while thy hook
    Spares the next swath and all its twinéd flowers:
And sometimes like a gleaner thou dost keep
  Steady thy laden head across a brook;
  Or by a cider-press, with patient look,
    Thou watchest the last oozings hours by hours.

3

Where are the songs of Spring? Aye, where are they?
   Think not of them, thou hast thy music too –
While barréd clouds bloom the soft-dying day,
   And touch the stubble-plains with rosy hue;
Then in a wailful choir the small gnats mourn
     Among the river sallows, borne aloft
       Or sinking as the light wind lives or dies;
And full-grown lambs loud bleat from hilly bourn;
     Hedge crickets sing; and now with treble soft
     The redbreast whistles from a garden-croft;
       And gathering swallows twitter in the skies.

―――――――――――

This poem was composed in September 1819 after Keats had taken a Sunday walk. It has been considered one of his best, and most mature. It is descriptive and can be seen as a kind of tribute to Ceres, the Roman goddess of the harvest. The autumn is seen as a time when one accepts the death of summer, although the poem suggests a kind of consolation.

RAINER MARIA RILKE
1875–1926

The Panther

Always passing bars has dulled
His sight so, it will hold no more.
For him, there are a thousand bars;
Behind the thousand bars, no world.

The soft walk of his strong, lithe strides
Turns in the smallest of all orbits
Like the dance of force around an axis
Where a great will stands stupefied.

Only sometimes, the curtain of his eye
Lifts, noiselessly – an image enters,
That runs through his tense, arrested members
Into the heart, to die.

(trans. W.D. Snodgrass)

LEWIS CARROLL
1832–1898

Lines from Mad Gardener's Song

He thought he saw an Elephant,
   That practised on a fife:
He looked again, and found it was
   A letter from his wife.
'At length I realize,' he said,
   'The bitterness of Life!'

He thought he saw a Buffalo
   Upon the chimney-piece:
He looked again, and found it was
   His Sister's Husband's Niece.
'Unless you leave this house,' he said,
   'I'll send for the Police!'

PERCY BYSSHE SHELLEY
1792–1822

Mutability

1

The flower that smiles today
　　　Tomorrow dies;
All that we wish to stay,
　　　Tempts and then flies.
What is this world's delight?
Lightning that mocks the night,
　　Brief even as bright.

2

Virtue, how frail it is!
　　　Friendship how rare!
Love, how it sells poor bliss
　　　For proud despair!
But we, though soon they fall,
Survive their joy and all
　　Which ours we call.

3
Whilst skies are blue and bright,
    Whilst flowers are gay,
Whilst eyes that change ere night
    Make glad the day,
Whilst yet the calm hours creep,
Dream thou – and from thy sleep
    Then wake to weep.

———————

This poem reminds us that change is the most constant thing in life.

EDMUND WALLER
1607–1687

Song

Go, lovely rose!
Tell her that wastes her time and me
That now she knows,
When I resemble her to thee,
How sweet and fair she seems to be.

Tell her that's young,
And shuns to have her graces spied,
That hadst thou sprung
In deserts, where no men abide,
Thou must have uncommended died.

Small is the worth
Of beauty from the light retired;
Bid her come forth,
Suffer herself to be desired,
And not blush so to be admired.

Then die! that she
The common fate of all things rare
May read in thee;
How small a part of time they share
That are so wondrous sweet and fair!

ALFRED, LORD TENNYSON
1809–1892

Lines from The Brook

I come from haunts of coot and hern,
    I make a sudden sally
And sparkle out among the fern,
    To bicker down a valley.

By thirty hills I hurry down,
    Or slip between the ridges,
By twenty thorps, a little town,
    And half a hundred bridges.

Till last by Philip's farm I flow
    To join the brimming river,
For men may come and men may go,
    But I go on for ever.

I chatter over stony ways,
    In little sharps and trebles,
I bubble into eddying bays,
    I babble on the pebbles.

With many a curve my banks I fret
    By many a field and fallow,
And many a fairy foreland set
    With willow-weed and mallow.

I chatter, chatter, as I flow
    To join the brimming river,
For men may come and men may go
    But I go on for ever.

WILLIAM SHAKESPEARE
1564-1616

Ariel's Song

Full fathom five thy father lies;
          Of his bones are coral made;
Those are pearls that were his eyes;
          Nothing of him that doth fade
But doth suffer a sea-change
Sea-nymphs hourly ring his knell:
          Burden. Ding-dong.
Hark! now I hear them – Ding-dong
          bell.

ALGERNON CHARLES SWINBURNE
1837–1909

The Garden of Proserpine

Here, where the world is quiet;
  Here, where all trouble seems
Dead winds' and spent waves' riot
  In doubtful dreams of dreams;
I watch the green field growing
For reaping folk and sowing,
For harvest-time and mowing,
  A sleepy world of streams.

I am tired of tears and laughter,
  And men that laugh and weep;
Of what may come hereafter
  For men that sow to reap:
I am weary of days and hours,
Blown buds of barren flowers,
Desires and dreams and powers
  And everything but sleep.

Here life has death for neighbor,
  And far from eye or ear
Wan waves and wet winds labor,
  Weak ships and spirits steer;
They drive adrift, and whither
They wot not who make thither;
But no such winds blow hither,
  And no such things grow here.

No growth of moor or coppice,
  No heather-flower or vine,
But bloomless buds of poppies,
  Green grapes of Proserpine,
Pale beds of blowing rushes
Where no leaf blooms or blushes
Save this whereout she crushes
  For dead men deadly wine.

Pale, without name or number,
　　In fruitless fields of corn,
They bow themselves and slumber
　　All night till light is born;
And like a soul belated,
In hell and heaven unmated,
By cloud and mist abated
　　Comes out of darkness morn.

Though one were strong as seven,
　　He too with death shall dwell,
Nor wake with wings in heaven,
　　Nor weep for pains in hell;
Though one were fair as roses,
His beauty clouds and closes;
And well though love reposes,
　　In the end it is not well.

Pale, beyond porch and portal,
　　Crowned with calm leaves, she stands
Who gathers all things mortal
　　With cold immortal hands;
Her languid lips are sweeter
Than love's who fears to greet her
To men that mix and meet her
　　From many times and lands.

She waits for each and other,
　　She waits for all men born;
Forgets the earth her mother,
　　The life of fruits and corn;
And spring and seed and swallow
Take wing for her and follow
Where summer song rings hollow
　　And flowers are put to scorn.

There go the loves that wither,
　　The old loves with wearier wings;
And all dead years draw thither,
　　And all disastrous things;
Dead dreams of days forsaken,
Blind buds that snows have shaken,
Wild leaves that winds have taken,
　　Red strays of ruined springs.

We are not sure of sorrow,
　And joy was never sure;
Today will die tomorrow;
　Time stoops to no man's lure;
And love, grown faint and fretful,
With lips but half regretful
Sighs, and with eyes forgetful
　Weeps that no love endure.

Swinburne was a religious and political radical whose ideas were considered shocking in his day. He disliked royalty, Christianity and any regime which he thought restricted people's freedom. He wanted to revive a pagan spirit in England and thought that artistic work should be decadent and provocative. He is remembered for drinking too much brandy and for poems, which have a lively, musical rhythm.

Proserpine is the Roman name for the Greek goddess Persephone, who was captured by Pluto to become his wife in the underworld. The poem favours love over virtue, and reminds the reader that there is no immortality.

HENRY WADSWORTH LONGFELLOW
1807–1882

Hiawatha's Childhood

At the door on summer evenings
Sat the little Hiawatha;
Heard the whispering of the pine-trees,
Heard the lapping of the water,
Sounds of music, words of wonder;
'Minne-wawa!' said the pine-trees,
'Mudway-aushka!' said the water.
    Saw the fire-fly, Wah-wah-taysee,
Flitting through the dusk of evening,
With the twinkle of its candle
Lighting up the brakes and bushes,
And he sang the song of children,
Sang the song Nokomis taught him:
    'Wah-wah-taysee, little firefly,
Little, flitting, white-fire insect,
Little, dancing, white-fire creature,
Light me with your little candle,
Ere upon my bed I lay me,
Ere in sleep I close my eyelids!'

———————————

Hiawatha is the tale of a Native American hero. In Longfellow's time there was still much conflict between the Native Americans and the white Europeans who were resented for taking over land which belonged to the Native Americans. Longfellow tries to tell a story, in the form of a poem, which brings the two American cultural histories together. It is based not on real Native American history but on myths and traditions familiar to many cultures. Longfellow compared his Hiawatha character to the ancient Greek hero Prometheus, who stole fire to save the human race.

CHARLES OLSON
1910–1970

The Distances

So the distances are Galatea
                and one does fall in love and desires
mastery
        old Zeus – young Augustus

Love knows no distance, no place
            is that far away or heat changes
into signals, and control
        old Zeus–young Augustus

Death is a loving matter, then, a horror
           we cannot bide, and avoid
by greedy life

        we think all living things are precious
        – Pygmalions

           a German inventor in Key West
who had a Cuban girl, and kept her, after her death
in his bed
          after her family retrieved her
he stole the body again from the vault
Torso on torso in either direction,
        young Augustus
          out via nothing where messages
are
   or in, down La Cluny's steps to the old man sitting
a god throned on torsoes,
        old Zeus

WILFRED OWEN
1893–1918

Futility

Move him into the sun—
Gently its touch awoke him once,
At home whispering of fields unsown.
Always it woke him, even in France,
Until this morning and this snow.
If anything might rouse him now
The kind old sun will know.

Think how it wakesthe seeds—
Woke, once, the clays of a cold star.
Are limbs, so dear-achieved, are sides,
Full-nerved – still warm – too hard to stir?
Was it for this the clay grew tall?
– O what made fatuous sunbeams toil
To break earth's sleep at all?

WENDY COPE
b. 1945

New Season

No coats today. Buds bulge on chestnut trees,
and on the doorstep of a big, old house
a young man stands and plays his flute.

I watch the silver notes fly up
and circle in blue sky above the traffic,
travelling where they will.

And suddenly this paving-stone
midway between my front door and the bus stop
is a starting-point.

From here I can go anywhere I choose.

Index of Poets

Index of First Lines

Poetry Acknowledgements

The editors and publishers gratefully acknowledge permission to reproduce the following copyright material:

A.K. Press. 'It's Work', from *School's Out: Poems Not For School*, by Benjamin Zephaniah, © 1997. 'Hymn to the Sun' by Pharoah Akhenation, trans. by John Perlman. Harcourt Brace & Co. Ltd. 'Mirabeau Bridge' by Guillaume Apollinaire (William Apollineris de Kostrowitski) trans. by Richard Wilbur from *New and Collected Poems*. Copyright © 1988 by Richard Wilbur. A.P. Watt Ltd. 'The Lake Isle of Innisfree', 'When You Are Old' and 'The Second Coming' by W.B. Yeats, on behalf of Michael B. Yeats and 'If' and 'Mandalay' by Rudyard Kipling, reprinted by permission of A.P. Watt Ltd on behalf of The National Trust for Places of Historic Interest, or Natural Beauty. 'Vitai Lampada' by Henry Newbolt © Peter Newbolt. 'Colonization in Reverse' by Louise Bennett. Black Sparrow Press. 'The Trash Men' from *Burning in Water Drowning in Flame: Poems 1955-1973* by Charles Bukowski, © Charles Bukowski (1974), reprinted by permission of Black Sparrow Press. Bloodaxe Books. 'No, I'm Not Afraid' by Irina Ratushinskaya, translated by David McDuff (1986). Osip Mandelstam 'Lightheartedly Take From the Palms of My Hands' translated by James Greene, © 1977 from *Osip Mandelstam*. 'Warning' by Jenny Joseph, from *Selected Poems* (Bloodaxe Books, 1992) by permission of John Johnson Ltd. Carcanet Press Limited. 'Counting the Beats' and 'It Was All Very Tidy' from *Complete Poems* by Robert Graves, 'This is Just to Say' from *Collected Poems* by William Carlos Williams and 'Six Strings' by Federico Garcia Lorca, translated by Donald Hall. David Higham Associates. 'Do not go gentle into that good night' from *The Poems of Dylan Thomas* by Dylan Thomas, published by J.M.Dent. André Deutsch Ltd. 'The Cow', 'The Duck' and 'Requiem' from *Candy is Dandy: The Best of Ogden Nash*, (1994), reprinted by permission of André Deutsch Ltd. Durfour Editions Inc. 'Autobiography of a Lungworm' by Roy Fuller: from *Collected Poems 1936-1961* by Roy Fuller. Printed with the permission of Durfour

273

Strauss & Giroux, Inc. 'The Fish' from *The Complete Poems* by Elizabeth Bishop. Reprinted by permission of Farrar, Straus & Giroux, Inc.